QUICK
HOME-COOKED
MEALS

QUICK
HOME-COOKED MEALS

Letting Your Microwave Work For You

(in 30 minutes or less)

MARYANN ZEPP

Good Books®

Intercourse, PA 17534
800/762-7171
www.goodbks.com

Design by Dawn J. Ranck
Illustrations by Cheryl Benner

QUICK HOMECOOKED MEALS
Copyright © 1999, 2003 by Good Books, Intercourse, PA 17534
Revised edition 2003.
International Standard Book Number: 1-56148-290-0 (paperback edition)
International Standard Book Number: 1-56148-410-5 (comb-bound paperback edition)
Library of Congress Catalog Card Number: 99-046391

Library of Congress Cataloging-in-Publication Data

Zepp, Maryann.
    Quick homecooked meals: letting your microwave work for you (in 30 minutes or less) /
Maryann Zepp.
    p. cm.
ISBN: 1-56148-290-0 (paperback)   IBSN: 1-56148-410-5 (comb-bound)
    1. Microwave cookery. 2. Quick and easy cookery. I. Title.

TX832.Z48 1999
641.5'882--dc21   99-046391

Table of Contents

INTRODUCTION

About This Cookbook

Enough pre-packaged dinners. Enough fast-food and carry-out dishes. You want more control over your own and your family's eating.

But you still have only limited time for cooking. You'll be tempted to return to your old practice of picking up pre-cooked food on the way home—unless you can find recipes and hints that match your schedule.

Quick Home-Cooked Meals is a cookbook that will show you how to manage it all. It is a colleciton of recipes that are simple, tasy, nutritious, and fast. Most can be made in 30 mintues or less.

The recipes require little time, but they offer foods' finest flavors. (What's more, preparing dishes in a microwave means comparatively little clean-up!)

So stop thinking of your microwave only as a place to revive leftovers. Let it do its full work for you. And enjoy better tasting, more healthy eating.

(If you need to get re-acquainted with the features of your microwave as well as its timesaving options, be sure to browse the next few pages, along with the Menu-Planning Guide and Tips.)

May you discover many **quick, home-cooked meals** with these recipes!

The 18 Most Asked Questions By Microwave Users

1. **What is a microwave?**
   - It is a form of radiant heat similar to a radio wave.
   - It is about the size of a standard pencil.
   - It cannot penetrate metal.
   - It passes through paper, glass, and plastic.
   - It cannot be stored.
   - It does not produce a chemical change in food.

2. **How do microwaves cook food?**
   - They are attracted to water, sugar, and fat molecules, causing those molecules to vibrate.
   - That vibration creates friction which in turn produces the heat which cooks the food.
   - Microwaves create friction on the outside of the food.
   - The inside of the food is cooked by the heat being conducted from the outside in.

3. **How does a microwave oven work?**
   - Most microwave ovens are easily installed by plugging them into regular household grounded outlets.
   - An electrical current activates the magnetron tube which produces microwaves. These microwaves are either deflected by a mode stirrer fan or emitted directly onto the food which is turned by a carousel. Microwaves are also deflected off the metal walls of the oven.

4. **Are microwave ovens safe to operate?**
   - First review your operator's manual!
   - Usually there are three safety locks which must be engaged before the oven will operate.
   - There is no documented proof of injury from radiation from a microwave oven. (There are, however, many incidences of cooking injuries from hot fat and boiling water, regardless of the kind of appliance used.)
   - Microwaves cannot leak from the oven because the oven is a metal box.
   - Microwaves travel in straight line so they cannot go around angles to escape.
   - The U.S. Government has declared microwave ovens to be absolutely safe without reservations.
   - Wearers of shielded pacemakers face no danger in operating a microwave oven. If you have any doubts consult your physician.

- It is essential that only microwave-safe equipment be used in a microwave oven. All recipes in this book presume the use of microwave-safe utensils and containers, whether stated specifically or not.

  To test for safety, place a glass measure containing ½ cup of water into the microwave oven. Beside it place the container being tested. Turn the oven on High for 1 minute.

  If the water is hot at the end of the minute and the container being tested is cool, it can be safely used in a microwave oven. If, however, the container being tested is warm, it has absorbed microwave energy and may in time crack or break as a result.

5. **What should you expect from microwave cooking?**

- Speed—Generally foods will cook in one-fourth the time required by conventional cooking methods. There are many exceptions to this rule which will be discussed throughout the book.

- Coolness—Heat is created within the food so your kitchen will remain cool.

- Economy—You are using much less energy to cook the foods since the cooking time is shorter. In addition, you are using less electrical wattage than a conventional electric stove uses.

- Nutrition—More vitamins and minerals are retained in the food because of its reduced cooking time.

Furthermore, one need not add any or much liquid and salt which dissolve many food nutrients.

- Color—Foods retain their natural colors.

- Taste—Foods retain their natural flavors.

- Convenience—Food can be cooked in its serving dish. (Dishes that work in the microwave can also be cleaned in the dishwasher.) Many foods can be cooked in disposable materials like paper plates, towels, or napkins.

  There is no mess while cooking. There is very little cleanup. And many ovens feature programs which allow you to cook meals while you are away from home.

6. **What are some variables I should know about?**

- Density—This is probably the most important of all variables. The thicker and heavier the food, the longer it will take to cook. Density affects a food's cooking time and placement in the oven. For example, arrange chicken pieces so that the thicker ends are to the outside of the dish where they are hit first by the microwaves. When doing broccoli and cauliflower flowerettes together, place the cauliflower along the outer edge because of its higher density.

- Volume—The more food you have the longer it will take to cook. If you microwave one potato, all the microwaves concentrate on it. The number of microwaves in an oven remains constant, so if you microwave four potatoes, they share the microwaves, and the cooking time is considerably longer.

- Starting temperature—Unless otherwise specified, most directions assume the food to be cooked is at room temperature. If the food is colder it will take longer to cook. (For example, frozen green beans take longer to cook than beans at room temperature.)

- Moisture content—It takes longer to cook foods with large volumes of water. Both pasta and soup with stock bases require as much time in the microwave as on a conventional stove. They can be cooked in a microwave oven, but that method will not save time.

- Standing time—This is as vital to successful microwaving as the actual cooking time. Standing time finishes the cooking process by allowing the heat on the outside of the food to transfer to the middle. This takes place outside the oven (except for cakes,) and for certain foods requires the same amount of time as the cooking process. It takes four minutes to microwave a pound of hamburger and another four minutes of standing time to complete the cooking.

7.   When should foods be covered?

Most foods should be covered when placed in a microwave oven, for two main reasons: to keep the heat and moisture in, and to keep the oven clean.

If the finished product is to be dry, cover it with a paper product. Waxed paper will keep the heat in and allow the steam to escape. Use it when baking a cake. Paper towels or napkins will absorb extra moisture created in the microwave. Use them to wrap baked products, like breads and rolls.

Plastic wrap or glass lids keep in both the moisture and the heat. Use these to cover roasts and most other high protein foods such as eggs. Cover vegetables with plastic or glass to keep in both the moisture and heat, thus producing steam.

Heavy plastic bags work well for frozen vegetables. Never use a metal twist tie because it will start a fire. Products high in sugar, fat, or water will retain too much heat and melt the plastic.

Nylon cooking bags work very well for conventional as well as microwave cooking. They retain the heat and moisture, contain the mess, and make a very convenient package for preparing a meal in a bag. Try meals-in-one (a roast and vegetables, for example) or anything covered with sauces.

Because the microwaves hit the corners and any protrusions first, those areas tend to dry out. Aluminum foil can be used to shield areas that may cook too quickly. Use these coverings to protect the corners on square pans or protrusions like wings on poultry.

(Aluminum foil should be folded smoothly to prevent sparking. But it presents no fire hazard like twisties or conventional metal plates.)

8. Do I need to rotate the dishes or stir the food?

Most microwaves have either a mode stirrer fan or a carousel to prevent over-cooking as a result of "hot spots."

The recipes collected here indicate when to stir food, but it is important to understand why it is frequently necessary. Because food cooks from the outside in, scrambled eggs, for example, should be stirred so the uncooked center is moved to the outside.

If it is not possible to stir the food (such as breads or cakes), it may be necessary to rotate the container so that even baking occurs.

9. What cannot be done successfully in a microwave oven?

- Eggs in the shell will explode. But be sure to see the Egg chapter (pages 23-30) for ways you can cook eggs in the microwave.

- Foods in which steam is the leavening—such as angel food and chiffon cakes, soufflés, and popovers—will not work. Their short cooking time and lack of a crisp crust prevents them from developing a structure.

- Toasting or crisping—such as is needed for home-fried potatoes or French toast—will not occur naturally but can be obtained with some adjustments.

- Deep-fat frying is not recommended because of the temperature required, but pan frying is attainable with small amounts of fat.

- Be careful with anything having a high concentration of fat, sugar, or water, since these foods attract microwaves. Consequently they cook fast and their temperatures rise quickly. Examples of these foods are corn syrup, honey, and spaghetti sauce.

- Anything encased must be pierced in some way to allow the steam to escape. This includes packages such as a box or pouch, a natural casing on liver or sausage, skins on baked potatoes, and the membrane of an egg.

- Almost any food in a quantity of more than 6 to 8 servings cannot be prepared more quickly in a microwave oven than on a conventional stove or oven. The more food there is to be cooked, the longer the cooking time required to cook it.

10. What are power levels?

The power level refers to the amount of power being emitted from the oven. If you are using an 800-watt oven at full power, you will be using 800 watts. If you operate that oven at 50% power you will be using 400 watts. While some microwave ovens refer to percentages, others designate levels from "1" to "10," and still others use gradations from "Low" to "High." If your oven uses a scale from 1 to 10, add a zero to each figure to arrive at the percentage of power. If you have further questions, consult your manual to discover how much power you are using.

11. How do I choose the correct power level?

Use the same judgment as you do when cooking conventionally. The more quickly the food is to be cooked, the higher the power level. For instance, to boil water use "High," but to cook a roast use a lower power level so the meat gets done in the middle without overcooking on the outside.

A "High" (100%) power level is assumed in the recipes in this collection unless otherwise stated.

12. Why is there a temperature setting on a microwave oven?

A temperature setting is often used in conjunction with a Temperature Probe, which is a kind of thermometer. A Temperature Probe records the internal temperature of a food while it is cooking and automatically shuts off the oven when the temperature at which it is set is reached. A Probe records the food temperature and not the oven temperature. When cooking to the desired temperature be sure to always follow the recipe's instructions about covering the food and which power level to use. That will assure your food is fully cooked without being dried out.

13. What is a multi-stage program?

Microwave ovens can be programmed to do a multitude of cooking procedures automatically. Each oven has its own features which you can discover in your manual, but many ovens can be set to move through the following steps:

- **Frozen casserole—**
  1st Stage—Defrost
  2nd Stage—Cook
  3rd Stage—Hold until ready to serve

- **Baking—**
  1st Stage—Begin baking process slowly
  2nd Stage—Quicken process by increasing the power level
  3rd Stage—Pause and test for doneness

Power Levels by Percentage in a Microwave Oven	Power Levels in a Microwave Oven	Temperatures in a Conventional Oven
10% Warm	1	100°F
20% Low	2	150°F
30% Defrost	3	200°F
40% Med-Low	4	250°F
50% Medium	5	300°F
60% Bake	6	350°F
70% Med-Hi	7	400°F
80% Reheat	8	450°F
90-100% Hi	9-10	500°F

- **White Sauce—**
  1st Stage—Melt butter
  2nd Stage—Cook added ingredients
  3rd Stage—Stir to prevent lumping

Multi-stage programming is a convenience so you can do all your programming in one step. Many models have memories in which you can store your most frequently used programs.

14. **Will food brown in the microwave?**

Yes! Meats cooked for more than 10 minutes will brown naturally. During cooking, the fat on the outside caramelizes and turns brown. The higher the fat content, the faster the meat will brown. For instance, bacon browns in one minute.

There are commercial products on the market to aid in browning those foods which need a little help! There are also many items in your kitchen which will aid in browning. Depending upon the food, many spices can be used to attain a browned color—soy sauce, barbecue sauce, onion soup mixes, brown sugar, and corn syrup. But more about that in the recipe sections.

A Browning Dish is required for foods with very short cooking times that need to be crisp or brown.

15. **What should I know about reheating food?**

- Always cover main dishes tightly. Reheat on High, if they have been refrigerated, until steaming hot.

- Stir a main dish, if possible, during reheating. If that cannot be done, rotate the dish while it is reheating.

- Reheat meats and layered main dishes at 50%. Meats should never be cooked beyond their original doneness. Layered casseroles need to be heated through, yet they can't be stirred, so lower power and longer reheating time works best.

- Begin heating a frozen casserole on High for 5 minutes. Stir, if possible, then reduce power to 50% and continue heating until food is steaming hot.

- To reheat a plate of food, place the denser foods (or the denser parts) to the outside and the more delicate or porous foods to the center. Cover with waxed paper or plastic. Heat at 80% for 3 minutes.

16. **Do I need to buy new cookware for use in my microwave oven?**

No! Most households have an array of cookware that can be used in a microwave oven. Glass, paper, and plastics are safe. If you are uncertain about a particular utensil, place a styrofoam cup full of water and the piece of cookware in question in the microwave oven. Microwave on High for one minute. If the water gets hot and the cookware remains at room temperature, it is suitable for microwave cooking.

Avoid metal cookware because it will reflect the microwaves rather than letting them penetrate. Avoid metallic trimmed cookware because energy can become trapped in the metal trim and cause arcing which appears as sparks and can cause a fire.

Aluminum trays can be used if they are less than ¾ inch deep and the foil cover is removed from the top. (If a metal tray is too deep, the energy can become trapped inside and cause a fire.) But insert the tray back into its cardboard package before placing it in the microwave to avoid metal touching metal. Never place a metal tray directly onto a metal rack.

17   Why do some microwave ovens have a metal rack?

A rack is to be used only when there is not enough space on the bottom of the oven to accommodate all the food to be cooked, or when food needs to be arranged for a varied cooking pattern. These racks are specifically designed with proper spacing for use in particular ovens so the microwave energy can pass through to each level.

18.   How do I adapt my recipes for use in the microwave?

There are three basic ways to work at this:

1. Find a microwave recipe that is similar to your conventional recipe and use that instead.

2. Experiment! Because each kind of food requires particular handling in the microwave, it is best to consult the chapter in this book containing recipes and ingredients most like the one you want to convert. (For example, the introduction to Cakes on page 113 explains that less water and fewer eggs are needed in a microwave than in a conventional oven.) Be sure also to check a parallel recipe's instructions about covering the food and the proper power levels to be sure the food will not dry out or be over- or under-cooked. Use a Temperature Probe to be sure the food reaches an internal temperature of 150°F, thereby assuring that the food is fully cooked.

3. If all else fails, divide your conventional recipe's cooking time by 4, and experiment from there. You should understand that converting recipes or multiplying or reducing a recipe's stated yield is always a bit of a gamble. Remember that because the number of microwaves in an oven is constant, larger amounts take longer than smaller portions. Experiment carefully, then record your successful results in the white space on the appropriate page.

A Quick Guide to Microwave Equipment

Glass Measure

This term refers to glass measuring cups with handles, that have graduations indicating measurements. The graduations are handy since you can measure and cook in the same container. The handle is helpful for removing extremely hot ingredients from the oven. The bowl will become very hot, but usually the handle remains cool enough to handle. This is especially useful when making candy. A deep measure is desirable for cooking foods that have a tendency to boil over. When purchasing, look for 2-, 4- and 8-cup sizes.

Glass Pie Pan

These usually come in 9- and 10-inch sizes. Both have their advantages. Omelets and pies work well in a 9-inch pan. Casseroles and meat need the larger space offered in the 10-inch size. This is a very versatile piece of equipment that is inexpensive and found on most cooks' shelves. It can double as a shallow casserole which can be covered with either waxed paper or plastic wrap.

Glass Baking Dish

Rectangular baking dishes are used to prepare a variety of foods. Be sure to check the size of your oven before purchasing any. If your oven has a carousel be sure the dish can turn. Choose a variety of sizes so you can cook the appropriate amounts for your household, as well as for larger groups when you have guests.

Covered Casseroles

Many kitchens are well equipped with a variety of usable casserole dishes. (If you need to stock up, a complete set can be purchased for about $20.) Many have interchangeable lids and stack for easy storage. Round casseroles give more even cooking results. Shallow casseroles allow for better cooking patterns, since the microwaves do not need to penetrate through as much food.

Baking Ring

This is a relatively inexpensive piece that you will quickly find indispensible. It provides even cooking patterns since it is round, and with the tube in the center, it allows food to cook from the inside out as well. Use it for just about anything that you want to cook quickly and efficiently. To substitute for it you can invert a glass tumbler in the middle of a round 3-quart casserole.

Meat Rack

Meat racks are available in a number of styles, shapes, and materials. Their purpose is to elevate the meat from its cooking juices. This can also be accomplished by inverting a saucer in a dish and laying the meat on the saucer. Meat racks are usually very inexpensive and a worthwhile purchase if you plan to cook a lot of meat. They work especially well for bacon.

Browning Dish

If you choose to purchase only one piece of equipment, it should probably be a browning dish. They come in a variety of shapes, sizes, and materials. Be sure you know your oven size and how you plan to use the dish before buying one. Having two different sizes is handy—a small one for quick breakfasts and lunches and a large one that covers the entire floor of the oven for doing larger quantities of food.

Plastic versus Glass

Both have their advantages and disadvantages. Glass may break but cooks and cleans up well. Plastics are sometimes sensitive to extreme temperatures and will blister or melt. Plastic stains more easily than glass.

THE RECIPES

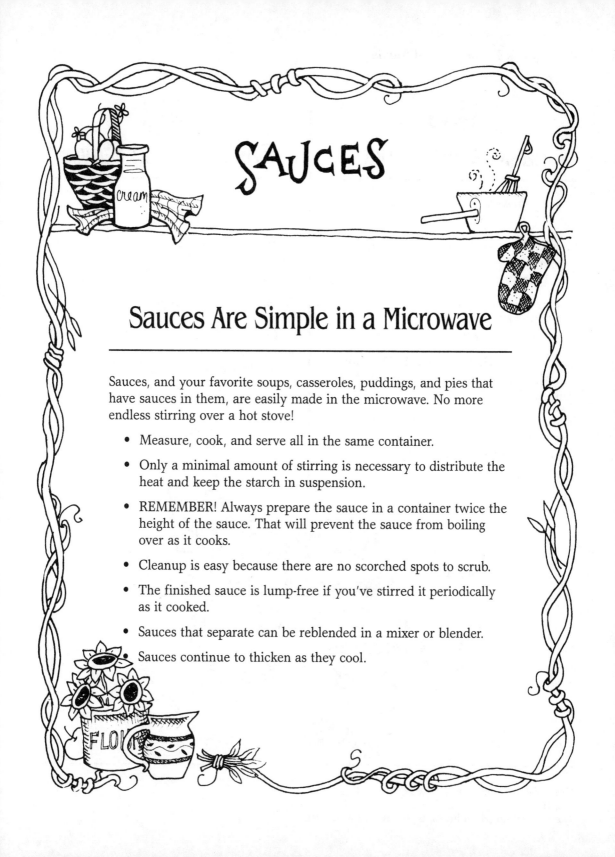

SAUCES

Sauces Are Simple in a Microwave

Sauces, and your favorite soups, casseroles, puddings, and pies that have sauces in them, are easily made in the microwave. No more endless stirring over a hot stove!

- Measure, cook, and serve all in the same container.

- Only a minimal amount of stirring is necessary to distribute the heat and keep the starch in suspension.

- REMEMBER! Always prepare the sauce in a container twice the height of the sauce. That will prevent the sauce from boiling over as it cooks.

- Cleanup is easy because there are no scorched spots to scrub.

- The finished sauce is lump-free if you've stirred it periodically as it cooked.

- Sauces that separate can be reblended in a mixer or blender.

- Sauces continue to thicken as they cool.

Basic White Sauce

Preparation Time: 5 minutes
Yields 1 cup

Microwave on High for 30 (25) seconds in a 4-cup glass measuring cup:
   2 Tbsp. margarine

Gradually stir in:
   2 Tbsp. flour
   1 cup warm milk

Microwave on High for 2:00 (1:40) minutes. Stir. Microwave on High another 2:00 (1:40) minutes. Stir.

Note: Constant stirring is not necessary because the microwaves agitate the liquid, but it is important to stir occasionally to avoid lumps.

Basic Cheese Sauce

Preparation Time: 5 minutes
Yields 2 cups

Prepare Basic White Sauce above. During final stirring blend in:
   1 cup cheese, shredded

Note: American cheese will give a creamy texture.
   Cheddar cheese will produce a rich color and flavor.
   A combination of cheeses works best and is a convenient way to use leftovers and ends that are beginning to dry out.

Note: This sauce works well over fresh broccoli and cauliflower or other vegetables.

Note: Each recipe indicates two cooking times.
The **first** is for a **650**-watt oven.
The **second** (in parentheses) is for an **800**-watt oven.

Brown Almond Sauce

Preparation Time: 10 minutes
Yields 1 cup

Place in 4-cup glass measure:
3 Tbsp. almonds, blanched
2 Tbsp. butter

Microwave on High for 2:00 (1:40) minutes, stirring twice during that time. Then stir in:
2 Tbsp. flour

Microwave on High for 60 (50) seconds. Gradually stir in:
1 cup light cream or half-and-half

Microwave on High for 2:00 (1:40) minutes. Stir. Microwave on High another 2:00 (1:40) minutes. Stir.

Brown Mushroom Sauce

Preparation Time: 10 minutes
Yields 1 cup

Place in 4-cup glass measuring cup:
3 Tbsp. fresh mushrooms, sliced
2 Tbsp. butter

Microwave on High for 60 (50) seconds. Stir. Microwave on High for 1 minute (50 seconds) more. Gently stir in:
2 Tbsp. flour

Microwave on High for 60 (50) seconds. Gradually stir in:
1 cup light cream or half-and-half

Microwave on High for 2:00 (1:40) minutes. Stir. Microwave on High for 2:00 (1:40) more minutes. Stir.

Note: Each recipe indicates two cooking times. The **first** is for a **650**-watt oven. The **second** (in parentheses) is for an **800**-watt oven.

Roux

Preparation Time: 2 minutes
Yields 4 tablespoons

Place in 2-cup glass measuring cup:
2 Tbsp. butter

Microwave on High for 30 (25) seconds.
Stir in:
2 Tbsp. flour

Microwave on High for 30 (25) seconds to take away the raw flour taste.

Note: *This can be whisked into any hot liquid to thicken it. Chicken, fish, beef, or veal stock make tasty gravies.*

White Sauce from Roux

Preparation Time: 5 minutes
Yields 1 cup medium white sauce

Heat in 4-cup glass measure:
1 cup milk

Whisk in:
4 Tbsp. Roux

Microwave on High for 2:00 (1:40) minutes. Stir. Microwave on High another 2:00 (1:40) minutes.

Note: *White sauce may also be referred to as Béchamel.*

Note: *For a richer sauce use cream instead of milk.*

Note: Each recipe indicates two cooking times.
The **first** is for a **650**-watt oven.
The **second** (in parentheses) is for an **800**-watt oven.

Cheese Sauce from Roux

Preparation Time: 5 minutes
Yields 2 cups

Prepare Béchamel or White Sauce as directed above.

Whisk in:
1 cup cheese, shredded

Season with salt, pepper, and dry mustard to taste.

Quick Sauces

Canned soups make very quick sauces. They can be served undiluted, or for a richer sauce they can be diluted with cream or stock. Pour into glass measuring cup and microwave on High for 3:00-6:00 (2:30-5:00) minutes. Processed cheese spread melts very quickly. It can be melted in its jar on High in about 60 (50) seconds (keep jar covered, but loosen its lid).

Mornay Sauce

Preparation Time: 10 minutes
Yields 1½ cups

Please in 4-cup glass measure:
2 Tbsp. butter
½ tsp. onion, minced

Microwave on High for 2:00 (1:40) minutes. Stir in:
2 Tbsp. flour
1 cup milk

Microwave on High for 2:00 (1:40) minutes. Stir. Microwave on High another 2:00 (1:40) minutes.

Gradually whisk in:
1 egg yolk
2 Tbsp. heavy cream

Microwave on High for 45 (38) seconds, stirring twice during that time. Stir in:
2 Tbsp. Parmesan cheese
¼ cup Gruyere or Swiss cheese, grated

Stir to melt cheese, then serve over eggs, chicken, fish, or vegetables.

Note: Each recipe indicates two cooking times. The **first** is for a **650**-watt oven. The **second** (in parentheses) is for an **800**-watt oven.

Hollandaise Sauce

Preparation Time: 4-5 minutes
Yields 1 cup

Note: *This Sauce has a tendency to curdle so be sure to microwave for only 15 (12) seconds at a time, then stir, alternating those steps until the Sauce is finished.*

In a small glass bowl combine:
3 egg yolks
4 1/2 tsp. lemon juice
dash red pepper sauce
dash white pepper

In 2-cup microwave-safe measuring cup, microwave on High for 45 (38) seconds:
1/2 cup butter

Whisk into egg mixture and microwave on High for 15 (12) seconds. Repeat the whisking and microwaving process 4 to 6 times, or until the Sauce resembles heavy cream. Season to taste with salt and serve immediately.

Note: *For an interesting twist, substitute 3 Tbsp. freshly squeezed orange juice and 1/2 tsp. finely grated rind for the lemon juice.*

Additional recipes in this collection which use Sauces or the techniques described here are:

Note: Each recipe indicates two cooking times.
The **first** is for a **650**-watt oven.
The **second** (in parentheses) is for an **800**-watt oven.

EGGS AND CHEESES

The Advantages of Cooking Eggs in a Microwave

- Prepare, cook, and serve all in the same container.

- One egg cooks in 45-60 (38-50) seconds!

- Eggs, properly microwaved, are light, fluffy, and moist.

- ALWAYS remove the egg from its shell and pierce the yolk before microwaving to prevent its exploding from internal pressure.

- ALWAYS cover an egg to trap the steam for even cooking and to protect your oven from splashes. A tight-fitting lid or plastic wrap produces the best results.

- It is best to microwave an egg at 70% power (rather than on High) since eggs are high in protein and so have a tendency to toughen at high temperatures.

- Don't overcook an egg. It should still look wet at the end of the suggested cooking time. Allow it to stand before cooking it longer. Because the cooking time is so short, you may need to experiment before finding the ideal cooking time for you. Make a note of what you discover works best.

Scrambled in a Cup

Scramble in a microwave-safe cup:
1 egg, yolk pierced
dash red pepper sauce

Cover with lid or plastic wrap.

Microwave at 70% for 60 (50) seconds. If the egg is not done to your liking, microwave in 10-second intervals until it is.

Note here how long it takes. _____

Season and serve.

Poached Egg

Place in 6-ounce custard cup:
¼ cup water
⅛ tsp. vinegar

Slip in:
1 egg, yolk pierced

Cover with lid or plastic wrap. Microwave on High (water absorbs extra power) for 60 (50) seconds. Season and serve.

Hard-Cooked Eggs for Slicing

Create your own round containers by cutting the cardboard cylinder from a paper towel roll into quarters, thus making four short cylinders. Line each with plastic wrap. Then stand each on end and break an egg into each container. Pierce the yolks with a wooden toothpick. Cover the top of each cylinder with plastic wrap. Microwave at 50% for 2:00 (1:40) minutes. Check for doneness.

If it is not necessary that the finished egg be round for slicing, crack the egg into a lightly greased custard cup. Cover with plastic wrap and microwave at 50% for 2:00 (1:40) minutes. Check for doneness.

Baked Egg

Place in 10-ounce custard cup:
½ tsp. butter, melted
1 egg, yolk pierced

Cover with plastic wrap. Microwave at 70% for 45 (38) seconds. Allow to stand for 1 minute.

Note: Each recipe indicates two cooking times.
The **first** is for a **650**-watt oven.
The **second** (in parentheses) is for an **800**-watt oven.

Puffy Omelet

Preparation Time: 25 minutes
4 servings

Microwave on High for 1-2 minutes
(50 seconds-1:40 minutes) in 2-quart
microwave-safe casserole:
¼ cup butter

Stir in:
¼ cup all-purpose flour
½ tsp. salt
dash red pepper sauce
1 cup milk, adding it gradually after
other ingredients are mixed in

Microwave on High for 3:00-5:00
(2:30-4:10) minutes or until bubbly. Stir
every minute during cooking time.

Stir in until melted:
1 cup cheese, shredded

Stir in:
1 cup chopped broccoli, cooked

Beat slightly and add slowly to vegetable
mixture:
4 egg yolks

Using clean beaters, beat until stiff peaks
form and then gently fold in:
4 egg whites

Microwave covered at 50% for 14:00-18:00
(11:40-15:00) minutes, or until set in the
center.

Serve warm.

Note: Substitute your favorite fillings. This is a convenient way to use leftovers.

Easy Omelet

Preparation Time: 7 minutes
2 servings

Combine in 9-inch microwave-safe pie
plate:
4 eggs
⅛ tsp. salt
dash red pepper sauce

Cover with plastic wrap. Microwave at 70%
for 4:00 (3:20) minutes.

Fill with favorite filling (see suggestions
below).

Microwave on High for 30 (25) seconds to
60 (50) seconds to warm filling.

Filling suggestions:
bacon, crumbled
broccoli and cauliflower, lightly cooked
cheese, grated
ham, cooked and cubed
mushrooms, sliced
onions and peppers, chopped
sausage, browned and crumbled
tomatoes, onions, and peppers,
chopped
any appropriate leftovers

Note: Each recipe indicates two cooking times.
The **first** is for a **650**-watt oven.
The **second** (in parentheses) is for an **800**-watt oven.

Croissant Breakfast Sandwich

Preparation Time: 10 minutes
4 servings

Beat together in 1-quart glass measuring bowl:
3 eggs
3 Tbsp. milk or water

Microwave on High for 3:00-3:30 (2:30-2:55) minutes, or until nearly set.

Cut in half horizontally:
4 baked croissants

Combine and then spread on each croissant:
2 Tbsp. mayonnaise
1 tsp. prepared mustard

Top with slice of:
ham or Canadian bacon

Spoon on egg mixture and top with other half of croissant.

Place on microwave-safe plate and cover with paper towel or napkin.

Microwave on High for 30-60 (25-50) seconds, or until heated through.

Denver Pockets

Preparation Time: 11 minutes
4 servings

Combine in 1-quart microwave-safe casserole:
1 small onion, chopped
1/4 cup green pepper, chopped
1 Tbsp. butter

Microwave on High for 2:00-3:00 (1:40-2:30) minutes, or until tender.

Stir in:
1/2 cup ham, cubed and cooked
3 eggs, beaten
1/8 tsp. salt
dash pepper

Microwave on High for 2:00-2:30 (1:40-2:05) minutes, or until eggs are set.

Cut in half to form 4 pockets:
2 6-inch pita breads

Fill each pocket with 1/2 cup egg mixture and sprinkle with:
shredded cheese

Microwave on High for 30-45 (25-38) seconds to melt cheese.

Note: Each recipe indicates two cooking times.
The **first** is for a **650**-watt oven.
The **second** (in parentheses) is for an **800**-watt oven.

Crab Quiche

Preparation Time: 30 minutes
6 servings

Combine:
1 cup unsifted all-purpose flour
½ tsp. salt

Cut in, until mixture resembles coarse crumbs:
⅓ cup shortening

In separate container combine:
2-4 Tbsp. cold water
2 drops yellow food coloring

Gradually stir into flour mixture until dough clings together. Form into a smooth ball.

Roll out onto floured, cloth-covered surface into a circle one inch larger than 9-inch glass pie plate. Fit into pie plate. Fold under edge, forming standing rim. Flute. Prick bottom and sides with fork. Weight with dried rice, beans, or a casserole dish. Microwave uncovered on High for 4:00-5:00 (3:20-4:10) minutes, or until crust is no longer doughy, rotating plate twice. Set crust aside.

Place in 1-cup glass measure:
1 cup half-and-half

Microwave on High 2:00-2:30 (1:40-2:05) minutes, or until steaming hot.

In separate container beat together:
4 eggs
1 tsp. chopped chives
1 tsp. dijon-style mustard
½ tsp. salt
dash pepper
dash nutmeg

Slowly beat in hot cream.

Layer in crust:
6 ounces crabmeat
¾ cup (3 ounces) shredded Swiss cheese

Pour egg mixture into crust. Cover with waxed paper.

Microwave on High for 7:00-9:00 (5:50-7:30) minutes, or until center is almost set, rotating dish two or three times.

Note: Other unbaked 9-inch pastry shells can be used. Prick with fork and microwave as directed. Frozen or canned shrimp can be substituted for crab.

Note: Each recipe indicates two cooking times.
The **first** is for a **650**-watt oven.
The **second** (in parentheses) is for an **800**-watt oven.

Pizza Quiche

Preparation time: 25 minutes
6-8 servings

Crumble into 9-inch glass pie plate, then microwave on High for 5:00-6:00 (4:10-5:00) minutes:
   1 lb. ground beef
   1 medium onion, chopped

Drain and stir in:
   1/2 tsp. salt
   1/4 tsp. pepper
   1 tsp. prepared mustard

Combine in blender and pour over cooked meat:
   1 1/4 cups milk
   3/4 cup buttermilk baking mix
   3 eggs

Microwave on High for 6:00 (5:00) minutes, or until edges are set; then microwave at 50% for 4:00-6:00 (3:20-5:00) minutes, or until center is set.

Top with:
   2 tomatoes, sliced
   1 cup cheese, shredded
   paprika

Microwave on High for 1:00-3:00 minutes (50 seconds-2:30 minutes), or until cheese is melted. Cut into wedges.

Serve warm.

Note: For more pizza flavor substitute 1 cup pizza sauce for tomatoes and microwave on High for 5:00-6:00 (4:10-5:00) minutes.

Quiche

Preparation Time: 20 minutes
6-8 servings

Microwave in glass pie plate on High for 4:00-5:00 (3:20-4:10) minutes, or until no longer doughy:
   9-inch pastry shell, pricked, and
      weighted with smaller dish

Microwave on High for 4:00-5:00 (3:20-4:10) minutes in glass bowl:
   1 small onion, chopped
   4 slices bacon, chopped

Stir in:
   2 Tbsp. flour
   1/2 tsp. salt
   dash red pepper sauce

Beat in:
   2 eggs
   1 1/4 cup half-and-half or light cream
   1/4 cup cheese, shredded

Pour into prepared pastry shell. Cover loosely with plastic wrap. Microwave on High for 6:00-8:00 (5:00-6:40) minutes, or until center is set. Let stand 10 minutes. Garnish with chopped chives or parsley.

Note: Each recipe indicates two cooking times.
The **first** is for a **650**-watt oven.
The **second** (in parentheses) is for an **800**-watt oven.

Sausage Quiche

Preparation Time: 25 minutes
6 servings

Microwave on High for 4:00-5:00
(3:20-4:10) minutes, or until no longer
doughy:
**9-inch pastry shell, pricked and
    weighted**

Microwave on High for 2:00-3:00
(1:40-2:30) minutes in microwavable
colander combination:
**1/2 lb. pork sausage, removed from
    casing**
3/4 cup fresh mushrooms, sliced
1/4 cup onion, chopped
1/4 cup green pepper, chopped
1 clove garlic, minced

Drain and sprinkle over bottom of partially
cooked pie shell.

Combine and pour over sausage mixture:
2 Tbsp. flour
1/2 tsp. salt
1/4 tsp. pepper
2 eggs
1 1/4 cups light cream

Top with:
3/4 cup mozzarella cheese
1/4 cup Parmesan cheese
2 Tbsp. fresh parsley, snipped

Cover with plastic wrap. Microwave on
High for 6:00-8:00 (5:00-6:40) minutes, or
until center is almost set.

Note: Each recipe indicates two cooking times.
The **first** is for a **650**-watt oven.
The **second** (in parentheses) is for an **800**-watt oven.

Swiss Cheese Fondue

Preparation Time: 15 minutes
Yields 3 cups

Combine in 1½-quart glass casserole:
3 Tbsp. all-purpose flour
¼ tsp. salt
⅛ tsp. white pepper
1 cup milk

Beat with rotary beater or wire whisk until
smooth. Stir in:
1 lb. Swiss cheese, shredded

Add:
1 Tbsp. butter or margarine

Cover with glass lid. Microwave at 70% for
5:00 (4:10) minutes. Stir well. Microwave at
70% for 5:00-6:00 (4:10-5:00) minutes, or
until thickened and smooth (about 180°F).

Stir in:
½ cup white cooking wine
dash nutmeg

Serve warm from fondue pot or chafing
dish with French bread cubes or bread
sticks. May be made ahead, refrigerated,
and reheated. To reheat, microwave at 70%
for about 8:00 (6:40) minutes, or until warm
(about 120°F). Stir well before serving.

Additional recipes in this collection which
use Eggs and Cheese and the techniques
described here are:

Note: Each recipe indicates two cooking times.
The **first** is for a **650**-watt oven.
The **second** (in parentheses) is for an **800**-watt oven.

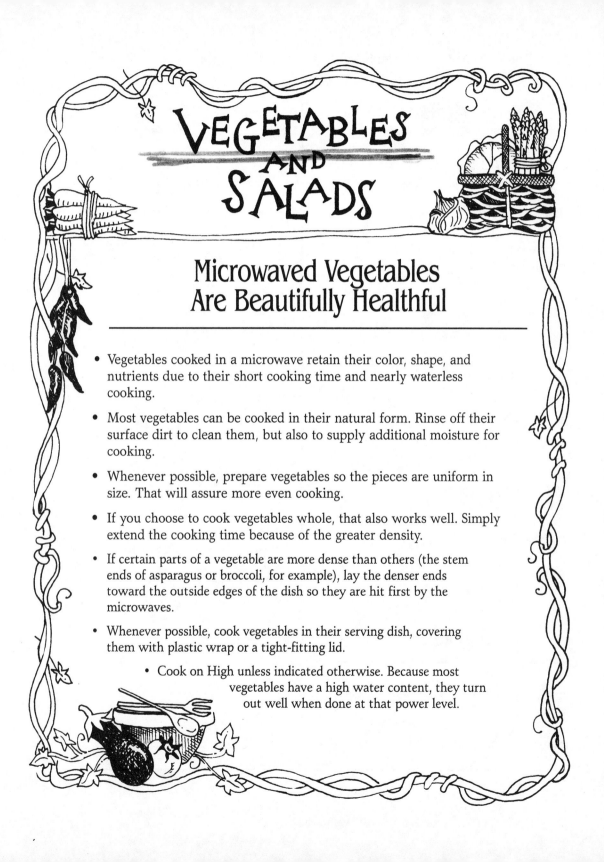

VEGETABLES AND SALADS

Microwaved Vegetables Are Beautifully Healthful

- Vegetables cooked in a microwave retain their color, shape, and nutrients due to their short cooking time and nearly waterless cooking.

- Most vegetables can be cooked in their natural form. Rinse off their surface dirt to clean them, but also to supply additional moisture for cooking.

- Whenever possible, prepare vegetables so the pieces are uniform in size. That will assure more even cooking.

- If you choose to cook vegetables whole, that also works well. Simply extend the cooking time because of the greater density.

- If certain parts of a vegetable are more dense than others (the stem ends of asparagus or broccoli, for example), lay the denser ends toward the outside edges of the dish so they are hit first by the microwaves.

- Whenever possible, cook vegetables in their serving dish, covering them with plastic wrap or a tight-fitting lid.

  - Cook on High unless indicated otherwise. Because most vegetables have a high water content, they turn out well when done at that power level.

Artichokes

Trim off stem and 1 inch off top. Brush with lemon juice. Wrap in waxed paper. Microwave on High for 4:00-6:00 (3:20-5:00) minutes apiece.

Asparagus

Due to its fibrous stems, asparagus needs water to cook. When preparing spears, stand them in a small amount of water and cover with plastic wrap, or arrange them in a circle lying flat, so the tips are to the center and the stems to the outside. Microwave on High for 6:00-8:00 (5:00-6:40) minutes per pound.

Broccoli

Fresh broccoli should be rinsed and cut into uniform pieces. Place in covered casserole and microwave on High for 5:00 (4:10) minutes per pound.

Beans (Green and Lima)

Beans require extra moisture for even cooking. Cover bottom of casserole with water, distribute beans evenly over top, and then tent with foil. This will cause the water on the bottom to steam the beans before the microwaves cook them on top. Microwave on High for 5:00-10:00 (4:10-8:20) minutes per pound.

Beets

Dice or slice into uniform pieces. Because beets are fibrous they require cooking in water or flavored juice. Place 1 pound in covered casserole with ¼ cup desired liquid and microwave on High for 5:00-7:00 (4:10-5:50) minutes per pound.

Note: Each recipe indicates two cooking times.
The **first** is for a **650**-watt oven.
The **second** (in parentheses) is for an **800**-watt oven.

Brussels Sprouts

Rinse sprouts and remove excess leaves. Combine 1 pound fresh sprouts in covered casserole with ¼ cup water. Microwave on High for 10:00-12:00 (8:20-10:00) minutes, or until tender.

Carrots

Dice or slice into uniform pieces. Because carrots are fibrous they require cooking in ¼ cup water or other liquid. Place in covered casserole with desired liquid and microwave on High for 5:00-7:00 (4:10-5:50) minutes per pound.

Cabbage

Shredded cabbage cooks faster than a whole head. Save the outer leaves for stuffing with a meat or vegetable mixture. Cut remainder of 1-pound head into wedges. Place in baking dish with ¼ cup water and microwave on High for 12:00-15:00 (10:00-12:30) minutes. Or shred cabbage, place in baking dish with ¼ cup water and microwave on High for 7:00-12:00 (5:50-10:00) minutes. To retain color, add a splash of lemon juice or vinegar to the cabbage before microwaving.

Cauliflower

Cauliflower can be cooked whole or broken into flowerettes. Rinse off surface dirt. Wrap in plastic wrap or place in covered casserole. Cook flowerettes on High for about 5:00 (4:10) minutes per pound. Cooking a whole 1-pound head on High will take 6:00-9:00 (5:00-7:30) minutes.

Note: Each recipe indicates two cooking times. The **first** is for a **650**-watt oven. The **second** (in parentheses) is for an **800**-watt oven.

Corn on the Cob

This is the easiest vegetable of all to prepare because it is in its natural wrapper. Just microwave in the husk on High for 3:00 (2:30) minutes per ear. Don't do more than six at a time. They will stay warm in the husk for 30 minutes while you attend to other matters. Be careful not to steam yourself when you husk them because they stay hot.

Corn Kernels

Place 2 cups kerneled corn in baking dish with 2 Tbsp. water. Cover tightly. Microwave on High for 4:00-7:00 (3:20-5:50) minutes.

Eggplant

For crisp eggplant, peel, then thinly slice it, dip each slice in egg wash and then into fresh bread crumbs. Preheat browning dish, add a small amount of oil, and brown to desired crispness.

Mushrooms

Wash and slice, chop or stuff. Saute with a small amount of butter by microwaving on High for 3:00-6:00 (2:30-5:00) minutes, stirring after 2 minutes. Or stuff with anything you like and arrange in a circle on a paper plate. Microwave on High for about 60 (50) seconds per plate.

Onions

Cook whole, sliced, or chopped. Onions are very flavorful when cooked mainly in their natural juices. Place 1 pound whole onions, along with 2 Tbsp. water, in 1½-quart casserole. Cover tightly. Microwave on High for 7:00-8:00 (5:50-6:40) minutes. Or place 1 pound sliced onions, along with 2 Tbsp. water, in 1½-quart casserole. Cover tightly. Microwave on High for 6:00-7:00 (5:00-5:50) minutes.

Note: Each recipe indicates two cooking times.
The **first** is for a **650**-watt oven.
The **second** (in parentheses) is for an **800**-watt oven.

Peas

Combine 2 cups fresh peas with ¼ cup water in covered casserole. Microwave on High for 7:00-8:00 (5:50-6:40) minutes.

Frozen peas cook very nicely in their box or pouch. Pierce and microwave on High for 4:00-6:00 (3:20-5:00) minutes for 10-ounce package.

Peppers

Peppers can be sauteed in their own juices. Rinse with water, remove stems, seeds, and membrane. Slice or chop to desired size. Place in microwave-safe dish and microwave to desired doneness. Start on High, checking every 30 (25) seconds for doneness.

Potatoes

A potato's size, type, and moisture all affect its cooking time. For example, a round potato takes longer to cook than an oval one.

Scrub potatoes to remove surface dirt. Pierce in several places to allow steam to escape. Arrange in a circle, spoke fashion. For a crisper shell grease the potatoes. Turn over halfway through cooking time for more even cooking. Microwave on High for 3:00-5:00 (2:30-4:10) minutes for each potato being cooked. Allow 5 minutes standing time. Potatoes will stay warm for 45 minutes if they are wrapped in foil or placed in a basket and covered. There are many uses for leftover potatoes:

- Slice or cube and brown in butter on browning dish.
- Cut in half and scoop out centers. Use for mashed potatoes or mix with cheese and bacon and restuff.
- Fill shells with creamed vegetables, chili, cheese, or other fillings.
- Cooked potatoes peel easily and are a good source of vitamins and minerals. They are extremely tasty when used in soups or salads.

Note: Each recipe indicates two cooking times. The **first** is for a **650**-watt oven. The **second** (in parentheses) is for an **800**-watt oven.

Spinach

Wash thoroughly, then cover, and microwave on High for 4:00-6:00 (3:20-5:00) minutes per pound.

Squash

Squash can be cooked whole, sliced, or diced. To cook whole, pierce skin in several places and place on paper plate. Microwave on High to desired doneness. You may want to partially cook it, then scoop out the pulp and finish cooking the pulp at mealtime. When preparing squash for freezing, cook until the pulp is tender, then puree it and freeze for later use.

Sweet Potatoes and Yams

Scrub and pierce skins of:
   5 sweet potatoes, 5-6 ounces each

Arrange in spoke fashion on round baking tray or plate. Microwave on High for 10:00 (8:20) minutes. When cool enough to handle, peel and slice into 2-quart glass casserole.

Combine in 2-cup glass measuring cup:
   1 cup brown sugar
   1/3 cup water
   2 Tbsp. butter
   1/2 tsp. salt

Microwave on High for 2:00 (1:40) minutes. Stir. Microwave on High another 2:00 (1:40) minutes. Pour over potatoes in casserole. Microwave on High for 6:00-8:00 (5:00-6:40) more minutes.

Note: Add your favorite ingredients to brighten the flavor: raisins, chopped apples, nuts, marshmallows, pineapples, or apricots.

Note: Each recipe indicates two cooking times.
The **first** is for a **650**-watt oven.
The **second** (in parentheses) is for an **800**-watt oven.

When Blanching Vegetables

- Use top quality vegetables.
- Clean and prepare as for cooking.
- Cut into uniform pieces.
- Blanch in container without water (and thus avoid the mess of draining).
- Chill in same container.
- Seal, label, date, and freeze.
- Reheat in same container.

Blanching Chart

Vegetable	Amount	Time
Asparagus (cut in 1-inch pieces)	4 cups	4:30 (3:45) minutes in ¼ cup water
Beans	1 pound	5:00 (4:10) minutes
Broccoli (cut in 2-inch pieces)	1 pound	5:30 (4:35) minutes
Carrots (sliced)	1 pound	5:00 (4:10) minutes
Cauliflower (flowerettes)	1 head	6:00 (5:00) minutes
Corn (cut from cob)	4 cups	4:00 (3:20) minutes
Peas	4 cups	4:30 (3:45) minutes
Spinach (washed)	1 pound	4:30 (3:45) minutes
Zucchini (sliced or cubed)	1 pound	4:30 (3:20) minutes

Note: Each recipe indicates two cooking times. The **first** is for a **650**-watt oven. The **second** (in parentheses) is for an **800**-watt oven.

Green Bean Bake

Preparation Time: 15 minutes
4 servings

Combine in 2-quart casserole:
   20 ounces frozen frenched green
   beans
   1 can condensed cream of mushroom
   soup

Cover and microwave on High for 9:00
(7:30) minutes.

Stir in:
   1 can french-fried onion rings
   (reserve a few for garnish)

Microwave on High for 3:00 (2:30) minutes.

Baked Beans
a la Microwave

Preparation Time: 15 minutes
6-8 servings

Place in 1½-quart glass casserole, cover
with paper towel, and microwave on High
for 4:00 (3:20) minutes, or until crisp:
   4 slices bacon

Remove bacon and crumble.

Stir into drippings, along with crumbled
bacon:
   1 cup catsup
   2 cans beans (mix any you like)
   ½ cup brown sugar
   1 Tbsp. prepared mustard
   1 Tbsp. Worcestershire sauce

Cover. Microwave on High for 7:00-8:00
(5:50-6:40) minutes, or until heated through.

Canned Beans
with Pork

Preparation Time: 6 minutes
2-3 servings

Place contents of 16-oz. can in covered
casserole and microwave on High for
4:00-6:00 (3:20-5:00) minutes.

Note: Each recipe indicates two cooking times.
The **first** is for a **650**-watt oven.
The **second** (in parentheses) is for an **800**-watt oven.

Broccoli and Cauliflower with Cheese Sauce

Preparation Time: 20 minutes
6-8 servings

Arrange on 10-inch glass baking platter:
1 lb. cauliflower flowerettes
1 lb. broccoli flowerettes

Decorate with:
red pepper rings, or
pimento, or
cherry tomatoes

Cover with plastic wrap. Microwave on High for 10:00-12:00 (8:20-10:00) minutes. Immediately uncover, being careful of steam.

Prepare Cheese Sauce by microwaving in 4-cup glass measure for 30 (25) seconds:
2 Tbsp. margarine

Stir in:
2 Tbsp. flour
1 cup warm milk

Microwave on High for 2:00 (1:40) minutes. Stir. Microwave on High for 2:00 (1:40) more minutes. Stir in:
1 cup cheddar cheese, shredded

Pour over broccoli and cauliflower.

Note: Add white sauce (page 18) to leftovers to create a cream soup, or add a package of stuffing mix and white sauce to leftovers to make a casserole.

Broccoli and Cauliflower Italiano

Preparation Time: 15 minutes
6-8 servings

Arrange on 10-inch glass baking platter:
1 lb. cauliflower flowerettes
1 lb. broccoli flowerettes

Decorate with:
red pepper rings, or
pimento, or
cherry tomatoes

Top with:
Italian dressing

Cover with plastic wrap and microwave on High for 10:00-12:00 (8:20-10:00) minutes.

Note: Each recipe indicates two cooking times. The **first** is for a **650**-watt oven. The **second** (in parentheses) is for an **800**-watt oven.

Eggplant Parmesan

Preparation Time: 20 minutes
6 servings

Combine in small bowl:
¼ cup bread crumbs
¼ cup Parmesan cheese
2 Tbsp. butter, melted

Layer in 1½-quart casserole:
1 medium eggplant, sliced and peeled
bread crumb mixture
2 cups spaghetti sauce (see page 70)
2 cups mozzarella cheese, grated

Cover with casserole lid and microwave on High to internal temperature of 150°F, about 15:00 (12:30) minutes.

Sausage-Stuffed Mushrooms

Preparation Time: 20 minutes
Yields 25-30 mushrooms

Wash:
1 lb. large fresh mushrooms

Twist stems from each cap.

Crumble into glass casserole:
1 lb. Italian sausage

Microwave on High for 4:00 (3:20) minutes. Drain. Combine sausage with:
8 ounces cream cheese, softened

Fill each mushroom with sausage mixture. Arrange stuffed mushroom caps on heat-resistant platter or paper plate. Microwave at 70% for 5:00-6:00 (4:10-5:00) minutes, or until hot. Serve hot.

Note: Each recipe indicates two cooking times.
The **first** is for a **650**-watt oven.
The **second** (in parentheses) is for an **800**-watt oven.

Stuffed Peppers

Preparation Time: 30 minutes
6 servings

Cut off tops and remove center from:
6 medium-sized peppers

In mixing bowl combine:
1 lb. ground beef
1 small onion, chopped
1 cup rice, uncooked
2 cups tomato sauce
2 cups water

Stuff peppers, mounding with filling.

Place in deep 3-quart casserole with lid.

Microwave at 80% about 25:00 (20:50) minutes, or until peppers are tender and filling is set.

Mashed Potatoes

Pare and cube potatoes, add a small amount of water, cover tightly, and microwave on High for 3:00 (2:30) minutes for each medium-sized potato. Season with salt, pepper, and butter. Mash to desired consistency, adding warmed milk.

Scalloped Potatoes

Butter casserole, layer sliced potatoes with butter, salt, and pepper, then cover and microwave on High for 3:00 (2:30) minutes for each medium potato used, or until potatoes are tender.

Scalloped Potatoes with White Sauce

Precook potatoes. Slice and layer in buttered casserole. Pour Basic White Sauce (see page 18) or Cheese Sauce (see page 18) over potatoes and microwave at 70% for 4:00-6:00 (3:20-5:00) minutes, or until potatoes are heated through. For a crisp crust, top with buttered bread crumbs or crushed cereal crumbs. Be sure to use an extra large casserole to prevent cooking over.

Note: Each recipe indicates two cooking times.
The **first** is for a **650**-watt oven.
The **second** (in parentheses) is for an **800**-watt oven.

Scalloped Potatoes and Ham

Combine in covered 1½-quart casserole, then microwave on High for 8:00-9:00 (6:40-7:30) minutes:

    4 cups potatoes, sliced
    1 small onion, sliced
    ½ cup water

Melt in 4-cup glass measure on High for 30 (25) seconds:
    2 Tbsp. butter

Stir in:
    2 Tbsp. flour
    1 cup milk, added gradually
    1 tsp. parsley
    ½ tsp. salt
    ¼ tsp. dry mustard
    ⅛ tsp. pepper

Microwave on High for 2:00 (1:40) minutes. Stir. Microwave on High another 2:00 (1:40) minutes. Stir in:
    1 cup cubed ham

Pour over potatoes. Sprinkle with paprika. Microwave on High for 5:00-6:00 (4:10-5:00) minutes.

Potato Brunch

Preparation Time: 15 minutes
6 servings

Place in shallow 2-quart covered casserole dish and microwave on High for 6-7 (5:00-5:50) minutes:

    12-ounce package hash browns

Combine in 1-quart glass measure and pour over potatoes:
    6 eggs
    ⅓ cup whipping cream
    1 cup cheddar cheese, grated
    2 Tbsp. chives, chopped
    ¼ tsp. salt
    dash pepper
    1 cup ham, cubed

Microwave on High for 3:00-4:00 (2:30-3:20) minutes. Stir. Microwave 2:00 (1:40) more minutes. Stir. Microwave again until eggs are set, being careful not to overcook them.

Note: Other fully-cooked meats can be substituted for ham, such as Canadian bacon, cooked pork roll, or cooked sausage.

Note: Each recipe indicates two cooking times.
The **first** is for a **650**-watt oven.
The **second** (in parentheses) is for an **800**-watt oven.

Potato Stuffing

Preparation Time: 15 minutes
4 servings

Combine in 9 x 13 baking dish:
½ cup butter
1 small onion, chopped

Microwave on High for 2:00 (1:40) minutes.
Add:
4 potatoes, peeled and cubed

Cover with plastic wrap and microwave on
High for 10:00 (8:20) minutes. Stir in:
2 cups croutons or stuffing mix

Stuffed Tomatoes

Cut tops off and scoop out:
6 medium tomatoes

Chop the centers and combine with:
1 cup bread crumbs
2 eggs
½ cup butter, melted
1 Tbsp. parsley, minced
1 Tbsp. onion, minced
1 tsp. paprika
salt and pepper to taste

Stuff, mounding filling into tomatoes.
Arrange in circle on microwave-safe platter.

Microwave at 70% for about 10:00 (8:20)
minutes, or until stuffing is puffy. Do not
overcook.

Greek Salad

Preparation Time: 20 minutes
8 servings

Microwave **1 lemon** on High for 20 (17)
seconds before squeezing to release more
juice.

Combine:
½ cup plain yogurt
½ cup mayonnaise
1 Tbsp. fresh lemon juice
1 tsp. dill

Pour over:
8 cups mixed greens
1 red onion, sliced
½ cucumber, sliced
1 tomato, chopped
½ cup feta cheese
¼ cup olives, sliced

Note: Each recipe indicates two cooking times.
The **first** is for a **650**-watt oven.
The **second** (in parentheses) is for an **800**-watt oven.

Antipasto Jar

Preparation Time: 30 minutes
Yields 10-12 cups

Microwave on High for 4:00 (3:20) minutes. Stir, then microwave on High another 4:00-6:00 (3:20-5:00) minutes, or until pickling liquid boils:

2 cups water
1 cup cider vinegar
2 Tbsp. salt
2 Tbsp. vegetable oil

Set pickling liquid aside.

Select 6 cups fresh vegetables:
broccoli, sliced
brussels sprouts, halved
carrots, sliced
cauliflower, sliced
squash, sliced

Cover and cook on High for 4:00-8:00 (3:20-6:40) minutes. Chill. Then select 2 more cups fresh vegetables:
green peppers, sliced
olives
cucumbers, sliced
small mushrooms
cherry tomatoes

Mix with cooled, cooked vegetables and pack in canning jars. Pour pickling liquid over vegetables. Cover and refrigerate 2 to 3 days before serving. Store in the refrigerator no longer than 1 month. Take advantage of fresh vegetables and use as hostess gifts!

Potato Salad

Preparation Time: 40 minutes
10 servings

Scrub **6 medium-sized potatoes**, then pierce each in several places to allow steam to escape. Arrange them in a circle, spoke-fashion. Microwave on High for 20-25 (16:40-20:50) minutes, turning each over mid-way through cooking time. Let them stand for 5 minutes. Peel and cube. Mix gently with:

1 small onion, chopped fine
1 cup celery, chopped
1 tsp. celery seed
1 tsp. salt
4 hard cooked eggs, diced
(see page 24)

Fold in 1¼-1½ cups Potato Salad Dressing. (See page 45.)

Note: Each recipe indicates two cooking times.
The **first** is for a **650**-watt oven.
The **second** (in parentheses) is for an **800**-watt oven.

Potato Salad Dressing

Preparation Time: 10 minutes
Yield 2 1/2-3 cups

Mix together:
2 eggs, well beaten
3/4 cup sugar
1 tsp. cornstarch
salt to taste
1/4-1/2 cup apple cider vinegar
1/2 cup cream or evaporated milk
1 tsp. prepared mustard
3 Tbsp. butter

Microwave on High for 2:00 (1:40) minutes. Stir. Microwave on High another 2:00 (1:40) minutes. Stir. Microwave on High 2:00 (1:40) more minutes. Continue that process until mixture thickens. Then stir in until smooth:
1 cup mayonnaise

Note: You may not need all of this Dressing for a single batch of Potato Salad (page 44). Begin by folding 1 1/4-1 1/2 cups into Salad. Add more as needed. Refrigerate what remains for another batch, or for use with a Pasta/Macaroni Salad.

Spinach Salad

Preparation Time: 15 minutes
6-8 servings

Place in glass baking dish and cover with paper towel:
2 slices bacon

Microwave on High for 3:00 (2:30) minutes, or until crisp. Remove bacon. Save drippings. Crumble bacon, then toss with:
12 ounces fresh spinach, cleaned and torn into small pieces
2 cups lettuce, shredded
6 green onions, sliced
3 hard-cooked eggs, chopped

Top with dressing made by combining in 1-cup glass measure and microwaving on High for 2:00 (1:40) minutes:
1/4 cup mayonnaise
2 Tbsp. sugar
2 Tbsp. vinegar
bacon drippings

Note: Each recipe indicates two cooking times. The **first** is for a **650**-watt oven. The **second** (in parentheses) is for an **800**-watt oven.

Sweet and Sour Dressing

Preparation Time: 5 minutes
Yields 1 cup

In a two-cup glass measure, microwave on High for 15 (12) seconds:
1 Tbsp. butter

Add:
1 Tbsp. flour
1 Tbsp. prepared mustard
¼ tsp. salt

Blend well. Stir in:
½ cup sugar

Slowly blend in:
½ cup vinegar
1 egg, beaten

Microwave on High for 2:00-3:00 (1:40-2:30) minutes, stirring after each minute, until mixture becomes very thick. Cool and chill before using. Dressing can be thinned with fruit juice to serve on fruit salad.

Additional Recipes in this collection using Vegetables and the processes described here are:

Potato Soup, page 49

Bean Soup, page 50

French Onion Soup, page 50

Note: Each recipe indicates two cooking times.
The **first** is for a **650**-watt oven.
The **second** (in parentheses) is for an **800**-watt oven.

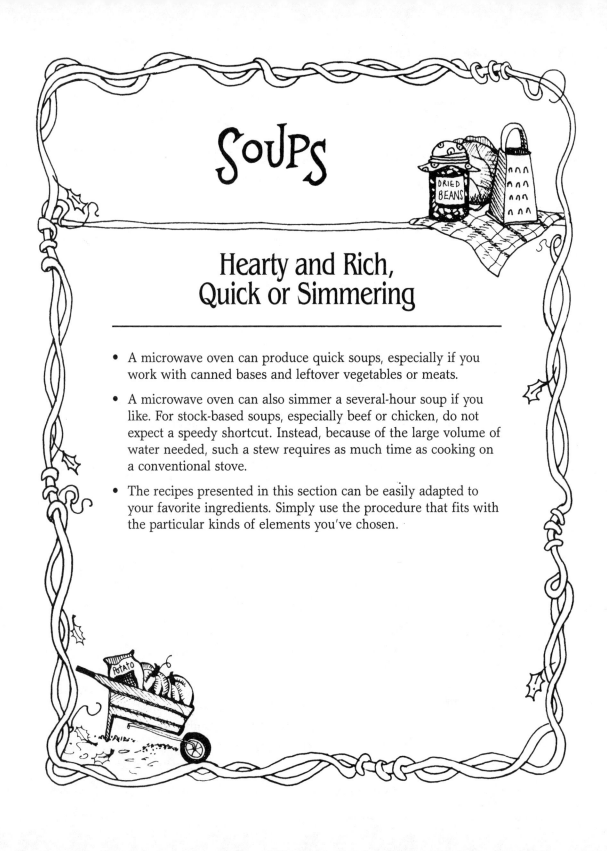

Soups

Hearty and Rich, Quick or Simmering

- A microwave oven can produce quick soups, especially if you work with canned bases and leftover vegetables or meats.

- A microwave oven can also simmer a several-hour soup if you like. For stock-based soups, especially beef or chicken, do not expect a speedy shortcut. Instead, because of the large volume of water needed, such a stew requires as much time as cooking on a conventional stove.

- The recipes presented in this section can be easily adapted to your favorite ingredients. Simply use the procedure that fits with the particular kinds of elements you've chosen.

Cream of Broccoli Soup

Preparation Time: 10 minutes
4 servings

Microwave on High for 30 (25) seconds:
2 Tbsp. margarine

Stir in:
2 Tbsp. flour
1 cup warm milk

Microwave on High for 2:00 (1:40) minutes. Stir. Microwave on High for 2:00 (1:40) more minutes. Stir in:
10-ounce package broccoli, defrosted

Microwave on High for 3:00 (2:30) minutes. Stir. Microwave on High another 2:00-3:00 (1:40-2:30) minutes, until steaming.

Hominy Clam Chowder

Preparation Time: 20 minutes
5-6 servings

Place in single layer in 2-quart glass casserole:
2 slices bacon

Cover with paper towel.

Microwave on High for 2:00-3:00 (1:40-2:30) minutes, or until crisp. Remove bacon and set aside.

Add to drippings:
1 medium onion, chopped

Cover with casserole lid.

Microwave on High for 2:00-3:00 (1:40-2:30) minutes, or until tender.

Stir in:
¼ cup flour
3 cups half-and-half

Add:
20-oz. can white hominy, drained
2 6½-oz. cans minced clams, undrained
½ tsp. salt
⅛ tsp. pepper
5 drops Tabasco sauce

Microwave uncovered on High for 9:00-10:00 (7:30-8:20) minutes, or until mixture boils and thickens, stirring three or four times. Garnish with crumbled bacon.

Note: 2 Tbsp. cooking oil or melted butter can

Note: Each recipe indicates two cooking times.
The **first** is for a **650**-watt oven.
The **second** (in parentheses) is for an **800**-watt oven.

be substituted for bacon drippings. A 16-oz. can of cut corn, drained, can be substituted for hominy. Chowder also can be made with half clams and half canned shrimp. Drain and rinse shrimp before adding to soup.

Potato Soup

Preparation Time: 35 minutes
4-6 servings

Place in single layer in 2-quart glass casserole:
3 slices bacon

Cover with paper towel. Microwave on High for 3:00-4:30 (2:30-3:45) minutes, or until bacon is crisp. Remove bacon and set aside.

Add to bacon drippings:
4 medium potatoes, cubed
1 small onion, chopped
1 cup celery, chopped
2 cups water
1½ tsp. salt
⅛ tsp. pepper

Cover with casserole lid. Microwave on High for 12:00-13:00 (10:00-10:50) minutes, or until vegetables are tender.

In a separate container, combine until smooth:
5 Tbsp. flour
2 cups milk

Stir into vegetable mixture. Microwave uncovered on High for 11:00-12:00 (9:10-10:00) minutes, or until mixture boils and thickens, stirring 2 or 3 times during the last half of cooking time. Crumble bacon and use to garnish soup.

Home-Cooked Chicken and Broth

Preparation Time: 80 minutes
Yields 5 cups broth, 4 cups chicken

Combine in 3- or 4-quart glass casserole:
3-3½ lbs. chicken pieces
5 cups water
1 large onion, chopped
½ cup carrot, chopped
½ cup celery, sliced
1 bay leaf
1 Tbsp. salt
⅛ tsp. pepper

Cover with casserole lid. Microwave on High for 18:00-20:00 (15:00-16:40) minutes or until mixture begins to boil. Rearrange chicken pieces. Cover.

Microwave at 50% for 50:00-60:00 (41:40-50:00) minutes, or until chicken is tender. Remove chicken and use as desired. Use broth for soups. If desired, skim fat from broth and strain to remove vegetable pieces.

Note: Each recipe indicates two cooking times. The **first** is for a **650**-watt oven. The **second** (in parentheses) is for an **800**-watt oven.

Bean Soup

Preparation Time: 2-3 hours
8 servings

Combine in 4-5-quart covered casserole:
1 lb. dried beans, washed and sorted
8 cups water
2 tsp. salt
2 tsp. baking soda

Microwave on High for 18:00-20:00 (15:00-16:40) minutes, or until boiling. Let stand covered 1 hour.

Stir in:
1 ham shank
1 large onion, sliced
1 bay leaf
6-oz. can tomato paste
¼ tsp. pepper

Microwave on High for 75:00-90:00 (62:30-75:00) minutes. Debone ham. Serve hot.

Note: This recipe freezes well.

French Onion Soup

Preparation time: 15 minutes
4-6 servings

Microwave in 3-quart casserole for 4:00 (3:20) minutes:
¼ cup butter
1 large sweet onion, thinly sliced and separated

Stir in and microwave on High for 4:00-6:00 (3:20-5:00) minutes:
20-ounce can beef broth
1 beef bouillon cube
1 tsp. salt
⅓ cup dry red wine (optional)
salt and pepper

Divide into mugs or soup bowls and top with:
melba toast rounds
shredded Gruyere cheese

Microwave on High for 60 (50) seconds to melt cheese.

Note: Each recipe indicates two cooking times.
The **first** is for a **650**-watt oven.
The **second** (in parentheses) is for an **800**-watt oven.

Country Minestrone

Preparation Time: 35 minutes
6-8 servings

Combine in 3-quart glass casserole:
  5 cups water
  10½ oz.-can condensed beef bouillon
  5 tsp. instant beef bouillon granules
  1 clove garlic, finely chopped
  1 small onion, chopped
  16 oz.-can tomatoes, undrained
  **1 cup broken, uncooked spaghetti
    pieces**
  1 tsp. salt
  ⅛ tsp. pepper
  ¼ tsp. oregano
  ¼ tsp. basil

Cover with casserole lid. Microwave on
High for 22:00-25:00 (18:20-20:50) minutes,
or until spaghetti is tender.

Add:
  1 cup frozen peas
  16 oz.-can kidney beans

Cover. Microwave on High for 5:00-6:00
(4:10-5:00) minutes, or until heated through.
If desired, sprinkle individual servings with
shredded mozzarella cheese just before
serving.

Sassy Tomato Soup
for Two

Preparation Time: 6 minutes
2-3 servings

Combine in 4-cup glass measure:
  1½ cups tomato juice
  **10½ oz.-can condensed beef
    consomme**
  ½ bay leaf
  dash of Tabasco sauce
  1 Tbsp. sugar
  1 tsp. parsley flakes
  dash pepper
  **½ tsp. Worcestershire sauce, if
    desired**

Microwave uncovered on High for
5:00-6:00 (4:10-5:00) minutes, or until
mixture begins to boil. Remove bay leaf.
Garnish each serving with a piece of celery
stalk.

Note: Each recipe indicates two cooking times.
The **first** is for a **650**-watt oven.
The **second** (in parentheses) is for an **800**-watt oven.

Notes

Note: Each recipe indicates two cooking times.
The **first** is for a **650**-watt oven.
The **second** (in parentheses) is for an **800**-watt oven.

PASTA, RICE AND GRAINS

Light, Fluffy Grains
Produced in Microwave

- Do not expect to save time cooking grains in the microwave. Because of the volume of water needed, the cooking time is about the same as on a conventional stove.

- Do expect lighter, fluffier finished grains, minimal cleanup, and energy-savings from your microwave oven.

- Do not expect to save time cooking pasta from scratch in the microwave. Because it, too, requires boiling a sizable amount of water, the cooking time is nearly the same as on a conventional stove.

Plain Pasta

For best results, microwave 6 ounces of spaghetti (or noodles or macaroni) in 4 quarts of water on High for 10:00-12:00 (8:20-10:00) minutes. Drain it, then rinse it to get rid of the starchy flavor. Mix desired Sauce (Spaghetti, Cheese, Cream, etc.) into it and microwave on High for 10:00 (8:20) more minutes, or until heated through.

Macaroni and Cheese

Preparation Time: 40 minutes
6 servings

Pour into a 4-quart microwave-safe casserole:
   4 cups water

Cover and cook on High for 8-12 (6:40-10:00) minutes, or until boiling.

Stir in:
   2 cups macaroni noodles, uncooked

Cover and cook on High for 2:00-4:00 (1:40-3:20) minutes, or until boiling. Stir. Cook on High another 2:00-4:00 (1:40-3:20) minutes. Let stand 2-3 minutes, then rinse to get rid of starchy flavor, and drain.

Pour Basic Cheese Sauce (see page 18) over cooked macaroni, then microwave on High for 5:00 (4:10) more minutes, or until macaroni are heated through. Set aside. Microwave on High for 45 (38) seconds:
   2 Tbsp. butter

Stir in:
   ¼ cup fine bread crumbs

Sprinkle over macaroni and serve.

Note: Each recipe indicates two cooking times.
The **first** is for a **650**-watt oven.
The **second** (in parentheses) is for an **800**-watt oven.

Fettuccine Alfredo

Preparation Time: 20 minutes
4-6 servings

Combine in 2-quart glass measure:
8 ounces dry fettucine
4 cups water
1 tsp. oil

Microwave on High for 10:00-12:00 (8:20-10:00) minutes, or until noodles are tender. Rinse with cold water and drain. Gently stir in:
1 cup half-and-half or light cream
½ cup Parmesan cheese
1 tsp. basil
½ tsp. salt
⅛ tsp. pepper

Microwave on High for 4:00-6:00 (3:20-5:00) minutes, or until heated through.

Note: There are excellent sauce mixes available for microwave use that include all the dry ingredients and require only the addition of milk and butter.

Pasta Primavera

Preparation Time: 40-45 minutes
6-8 servings

Combine in 2-quart glass measure:
8 ounces dry fettucine
4 cups water
1 tsp. oil

Microwave on High for 10:00-12:00 (8:20-10:00) minutes, or until noodles are tender. Rinse with cold water and drain.

Combine in 3-quart covered casserole:
2 cups broccoli, cut up
2 cups cauliflower, cut up
1 cup carrots, thinly sliced
1 medium zucchini, sliced
1 clove garlic, minced
2 Tbsp. water

Microwave on High for 11:00-13:00 (9:10-10:50) minutes, or until vegetables are tender. Drain and add to pasta, along with:
10-12 cherry tomatoes
1 cup half-and-half or light cream
½ cup Parmesan cheese
1 tsp. basil
½ tsp. salt
⅛ tsp. pepper

Microwave on High for 6:00-8:00 (5:00-6:40) minutes, or until heated through.

Note: Each recipe indicates two cooking times. The **first** is for a **650**-watt oven. The **second** (in parentheses) is for an **800**-watt oven.

Tuna Noodle Casserole

Preparation Time: 25 minutes
4-6 servings

Combine in 2-quart casserole:
  1 cup water
  1½ cups egg noodles, uncooked

Microwave on High for 5:00 (4:10) minutes.
Stir, then microwave again on High for 5:00
(4:10) minutes. Stir in:
  6-ounce can tuna
  1 can cream of mushroom soup
  ¼ cup mushrooms (4 ounces)
  2 cups peas (10-ounce package)

Cover with casserole lid. Microwave on
High for 5:00 (4:10) minutes. Top with:
  crushed potato chips or buttered
  crackers

Microwave on High for 4:00-6:00
(3:20-5:00) minutes, uncovered.

Long-Grain Rice

Preparation Time: 20 minutes
4-6 servings

Combine in a 2-quart covered casserole:
  1 cup rice
  2 cups liquid (water or broth)
  1 tsp. salt
  1 Tbsp. butter

Microwave on High for 5:00 (4:10) minutes,
or until mixture is boiling, then at 50% for
15:00 (12:30) minutes, or until rice is tender
and liquid is absorbed.

Brown Rice

Preparation Time: 1¼ hours
4-6 servings

Combine in covered 2-quart casserole:
  1 cup brown rice
  2½ cups chicken broth
  ¼ cup water
  1 Tbsp. instant onion
  ⅛ tsp. ground oregano

Microwave on High for 8:00-10:00
(6:40-8:20) minutes, or until mixture is
boiling, then at 50% for 45:00-60:00
(37:30-50:00) minutes.

Note: Each recipe indicates two cooking times.
The **first** is for a **650**-watt oven.
The **second** (in parentheses) is for an **800**-watt oven.

Micro-Fried Rice

Preparation Time: 10 minutes
4 servings

Combine in 1-quart microwave-safe
casserole:
   1 cup rice, cooked
   2 tsp. soy sauce
   3 green onions, sliced
   1 tsp. parsley flakes
   3 eggs, beaten
   1/2 cup water chestnuts, chopped

Microwave covered on High for 3-5
(2:30-4:10) minutes, or until eggs are set.
Stir before serving.

Spanish Rice

Preparation Time: 45 minutes
6 servings

Place in 1 1/2-quart casserole, cover with
paper towel, and microwave on High for
3:00-4:00 (2:30-3:20) minutes, or until crisp:
   4 slices bacon

Remove bacon and add to bacon drippings:
   1/3 cup onion, chopped
   1/3 cup green pepper, chopped

Microwave on High for 2:00-4:00
(1:40-3:20) minutes, then stir in:
   2 cups tomatoes, cut up
   1/4 tsp. celery salt

Cover and microwave on High for
3:00-4:00 (2:30-3:20) minutes, then stir
in until moistened:
   1/2 cup long grain rice

Microwave on High for 25:00-30:00
(20:50-25:00) minutes, or until rice is tender.
Sprinkle with crumbled bacon and:
   1/2 cup cheddar cheese, shredded

Microwave on High for 60 (50) seconds, or
until cheese is melted.

Note: Each recipe indicates two cooking times.
The **first** is for a **650**-watt oven.
The **second** (in parentheses) is for an **800**-watt oven.

Oatmeal

Preparation Time: 5 minutes
1 serving

Stir together, then microwave on High for
1:30 (1:15) minutes:
   ¼ cup dry quick oats
   ½ cup water
   pinch salt

Stir, then cover and let stand 2-3 minutes.
Serve topped with fruit or brown sugar and
milk.

Big-Batch Oatmeal

Preparation Time: 10 minutes
6 servings

Stir together, then microwave on High for
4:00 (3:20) minutes:
   1½ cups dry oatmeal
   3 cups water
   ¾ tsp. salt

Stir, then cover and let stand 5 minutes.
Serve topped with fruit or brown sugar and
milk.

Additional recipes in this collection which
use pasta, rice, and grains:

   Lasagna, page 66

   Chinese Casserole, page 68

   Ground Beef and Rice, page 68

   Pork Chop-Noodle Dinner, page 74

   Pork and Rice a L'Orange, page 74

   Ham and Cheese Casserole, page 76

   Rice and Sausage Casserole, page 78

   Sausage-Macaroni Skillet, page 78

   Chicken and Rice, page 86

   Chicken-Rice Bake, page 87

   Jiffy Tuna Casserole, page 104

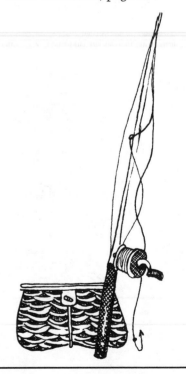

Note: Each recipe indicates two cooking times.
The **first** is for a **650**-watt oven.
The **second** (in parentheses) is for an **800**-watt oven.

BEEF

Microwaved Meats are Flavorful

- Meats should be completely defrosted before cooking.

- Whenever possible, defrost in original wrappings, removing any ties, rings, foils, or wires.

- Place package of unwrapped meat in a microwave-safe dish.

- Defrost on Low only until meat becomes pliable. Remove from oven and allow standing time to complete the process.

- Meats cooked for more than 10 minutes will brown naturally. The more fat on the surface of the meat, the browner the finished product.

- The browning process can be enhanced by using browning agents, steak sauce, soy sauce, or spices such as chili powder, pepper, or paprika.

Steak

Preparation Time: 10-15 minutes

For crisp surface:

Use browning dish. Preheat 2-10 (1:40-8:20) minutes depending on size of browner and manufacturer's directions. Grease dish with butter or margarine for better color. Depending on size of piece of meat, microwave on High for 2-5 (1:40-4:10) minutes on each side.

Preparation Time: 5-10 minutes

For moister, more tender surface:

Coat meat with favorite browning agent or seasoning (avoid salt). Place on meat rack. Cover with waxed paper. Microwave on High for 2:00-4:00 (1:40-3:20) minutes per piece. Turn over and repeat process.

Beef Roast

Place roast on roasting rack, fat side down.

Coat with browning agent, if desired.

Insert probe, being careful to avoid bone, fat, or air pockets.

Cover tightly with lid or plastic wrap, or place in cooking bag.

Shield with foil areas that have a tendency to brown too quickly.

Turn large pieces of meat over mid-way through the cooking process to insure consistent doneness.

Roast at 30-70% to desired internal temperature, testing at several places to be sure the correct temperature has been reached throughout:

Beef rare	120°F
Beef medium	135°F
Beef well done	160°F

Allow to stand 10 minutes.

Salt after cooking so the meat retains its moisture.

Carve and serve.

Note: Each recipe indicates two cooking times.
The **first** is for a **650**-watt oven.
The **second** (in parentheses) is for an **800**-watt oven.

Night-Before Pot Roast

Preparation Time: 40 minutes
6 servings

Combine in 9 x 13 glass baking dish:
1 pkg. onion soup mix
1 cup cooking wine
1/2 tsp. salt
1/4 tsp. pepper
2-3 lb. chuck roast

Cover with plastic wrap and refrigerate overnight. Turn over in the morning. Add:
4 small potatoes
4 carrots, peeled and quartered

Microwave at 50% for 35:00 (29:10) minutes, or to 150°F.

Beef Cubes

Preparation Time: 1 1/2-2 hours
6 servings

Combine in covered 3-quart casserole:
2 lbs. beef cubes
1 can beef broth (or 2 cups water and 2 bouillon cubes)
1 medium onion, chopped
1/4 tsp. pepper

Microwave on High for 10:00 (8:20) minutes, then at 30% for 90:00-100:00 (75:00-83:20) minutes, or until tender.

Chuck (or Less Tender) Roast

Preparation Time: 1-1 1/4 hours
6-8 servings

Coat nylon cooking bag with:
1 Tbsp. flour

Add:
3-lb. roast, fat side down
3-6 red potatoes, peeled
3-6 carrots, peeled and pared
6-oz. can tomato sauce
6-ozs. cooking wine

Insert probe in the center of the muscle.

Seal bag with nylon tie. Microwave on High for 10:00 (8:20) minutes.

Turn over. Insert probe and cook at 50% to 135°F.

Allow to stand 10 minutes.

Note: Each recipe indicates two cooking times. The **first** is for a **650**-watt oven. The **second** (in parentheses) is for an **800**-watt oven.

Beef Burgundy

Preparation Time: 26 minutes
4 servings

Combine in 2-quart casserole:
  **2 medium carrots, peeled and cut
    into 1″ pieces**
  2 cups beef cubes, cooked
  1 cup cooking juices or beef broth
  1/2 cup fresh mushrooms
  1 cup small whole onions
  1 clove garlic, minced
  1 bay leaf
  3 Tbsp. red cooking wine
  1 tsp. parsley flakes
  1 Tbsp. flour

Microwave on High for 15:00-17:00
(12:30-14:10) minutes, stirring once or
twice, or until carrots are tender.

Beef Stroganoff

Preparation Time: 12 minutes
4 servings

Combine in 1 1/2-quart covered casserole:
  2 cups beef cubes, cooked
  1 cup cooking juices or broth
  1/2 cup mushrooms, sliced

Microwave on High for 5:00-6:00
(4:10-5:00) minutes, or until mushrooms are
tender.

Mix together and add to meat:
  1 cup sour cream
  2 Tbsp. flour

Microwave on High for 2:00 (1:40) minutes.
Stir. Microwave on High another 2:00 (1:40)
minutes. Stir until thickened. Serve over
buttered noodles.

Cheesy Meat Loaf

Preparation time: 12 minutes
4 servings

Combine in mixing bowl:
  1 lb. ground beef
  **3 slices bread, moistened and
    crumbled**
  1 egg
  1 small onion, chopped
  1/4 cup catsup
  1 Tbsp. Worcestershire sauce

Pat into baking ring and top with:
  1/4 cup parmesan cheese

Cover with waxed paper. Microwave on
High for 6:00-8:00 (5:00-6:40) minutes.

Note: Each recipe indicates two cooking times.
The **first** is for a **650**-watt oven.
The **second** (in parentheses) is for an **800**-watt oven.

Meat Loaf

Preparation time: 15 minutes
6 servings

Combine in mixing bowl:
  1 lb. ground beef
  1/2 lb. ground pork
  1 envelope onion soup mix
  1 slice bread, crumbled
  1 egg
  1/4 cup tomato juice or milk

Pat into baking ring. Sprinkle with browning powder or onion soup mix. Cover with waxed paper. Microwave on High for 6:00-8:00 (5:00-6:40) minutes or to 150°F.

Defrosting and Cooking Ground Beef

- Defrost at 30% for 4:00 (3:20) minutes per pound. Then allow 5:00 (4:10) minutes standing time per pound to complete the defrosting process.

- To cook thoroughly, microwave on High for 5:00-6:00 (4:10-5:00) minutes per pound.

- To eliminate excess fat, cook ground beef in a microwave-safe colander set in a casserole dish or pie plate to catch the drippings.

- Stir ground beef once or twice during cooking time to break up the lumps of meat.

- To enhance the cooked meat's color, sprinkle it with a browning agent or seasoning mix before microwaving.

- For even cooking, bake meat loaf in a ring pan or in a casserole dish with a glass tumbler inverted in the center.

- For even cooking, arrange meat balls in a circle on a plate or in a casserole dish.

- Because microwave ovens can make cooking such a speedy process, we offer here recipes that capitalize on that efficiency. Packaged sauces and mixes contribute to quickly preparing food. On the other hand, "from-scratch" chili and slowly stewed spaghetti sauce can also be made in the microwave. They may take as long as they do on a conventional stove, but cooking them in the microwave is still an efficient method, cleanup-wise.

Note: Each recipe indicates two cooking times.
The **first** is for a **650**-watt oven.
The **second** (in parentheses) is for an **800**-watt oven.

To Prepare a Packaged Ground Beef Mix

Crumble into casserole:
1 lb. ground beef

Microwave on High for 5:00-6:00 (4:10-5:00) minutes. Drain fat and stir in:
**1 package hamburger mix
(7 1/2 ounces)
3 1/4 cups water**

Cover and microwave on High for 12:00-13:00 (10:00-10:50) minutes, or until noodles are tender.

Chili

*Preparation Time: 20 minutes
6 servings*

Crumble in 3-quart casserole:
1 lb. ground beef

Sprinkle with:
**1 1/2 tsp. chili powder
1 1/2 tsp. salt
1 Tbsp. flour
1 onion, chopped fine**

Or:
1 envelope chili seasoning mix

Microwave on High for 5:00 (4:10) minutes. Stir in:
**2 cups tomato sauce
2 cups kidney beans, prepared**

Cover with casserole lid and cook on High for 6:00-8:00 (5:00-6:40) minutes, or until the chili reaches an internal temperature of 135°F.

Note: Each recipe indicates two cooking times.
The **first** is for a **650**-watt oven.
The **second** (in parentheses) is for an **800**-watt oven.

Cranberry Glazed Loaves

Preparation Time: 22 minutes
4-6 servings

Combine in mixing bowl:
  1 egg, beaten
  1/3 cup milk
  1/3 cup dry quick cooking oats
  2 Tbsp. onion, finely chopped
  1/2 tsp. salt
  dash pepper
  1 lb. ground beef

Shape into 4 or 5 loaves. Place in a 9 x 13 baking pan and top with a combination of:
  1 cup whole cranberry sauce
  1 cup brown sugar
  2 tsp. lemon juice

Arrange loaves in circle and microwave at 80% for 12:00-15:00 (10:00-12:30) minutes.

Meat Balls and Tomato Sauce

Preparation time: 15 minutes
6 servings

Combine:
  1 lb. ground beef
  2 slices bread, torn into crumbs
  1 egg
  2 Tbsp. oregano
  salt and pepper ~~FINE ONION~~

Shape into meat balls and arrange in single layer in 3-quart casserole.

Cover and microwave on High for 4:00 (3:20) minutes. Pour over meatballs:
  1 jar spaghetti sauce or 3 cups Home-Prepared Spaghetti Sauce (page 70)

Cover. Microwave on High for 6:00-8:00 (5:00-6:40) minutes, or until heated through.

Note: Each recipe indicates two cooking times. The **first** is for a **650**-watt oven. The **second** (in parentheses) is for an **800**-watt oven.

Lasagna

Preparation time: 1¹/4 hours
10 servings

Nothing needs to be precooked to make microwaved Lasagna. You will not save much time but you will avoid a lot of mess. This dish works well when you have time to prepare it ahead of time or want to have something time-cooked while you are away.

Divide the following ingredients into 3 layers in a 9 x 13-inch baking pan:

Layer 1:
   9 lasagna noodles (use 3 noodles for each layer)

Layer 2:
   2 cups ricotta cheese (use ²/3 cup for each layer)
   1¹/3 cups Parmesan cheese (use ¹/3 cup for each layer, reserving ¹/3 cup for the top of finished casserole)
   1 cup mozzarella cheese, shredded (use ¹/3 cup for each layer)

Layer 3:
   1 lb. ground beef (use ¹/3 cup for each layer)
   28-oz. or 35-oz. jar of spaghetti sauce or Home-Prepared Sauce, page 70 (use 1+ cup for each layer)

Assemble layers, ending with spaghetti sauce. Cover with waxed paper.

Microwave on High for 10:00 (8:20) minutes. Simmer at 50% for 30:00 (25:00) minutes, or to an internal temperature of 150°F. Top with reserved Parmesan cheese. Microwave on High for 3:00-5:00 (2:30-4:10) minutes. Let sit for 10 minutes before serving.

Hamburgers

Form 1 lb. of ground beef into 4 patties, adding chopped onion, seasoning, egg, tomato juice, and bread crumbs, if desired.

To microwave burgers on a paper-lined plate or roasting rack, cover with waxed paper, then microwave on High for 2:00 (1:40) minutes to attain medium-rare burgers. (Microwave on High for 2:30 (2:05) minutes for medium-well-done burgers.) Turn burgers over and cover. Microwave on High for 1-2 (50 seconds-1:40) more minutes for medium-rare burgers. (Microwave on High for 2:00-3:00 (1:40-2:30) minutes for medium-well-done burgers.)

Allow to stand, covered, for 1-2 minutes to complete cooking and to attain a browner color.

To microwave burgers on a browning dish, preheat dish according to manufacturer's directions. Microwave on High for 2:00 (1:40) minutes for medium-rare-burgers. (Microwave on High for 2:30 (2:05) minutes for medium-well-done burgers.)

Note: Each recipe indicates two cooking times.
The **first** is for a **650**-watt oven.
The **second** (in parentheses) is for an **800**-watt oven.

Turn burgers over and microwave on High for 1-2 (50 seconds-1:40) more minutes for medium-rare burgers. (Microwave on High for 2:30 (2:05) minutes for medium-well-done burgers.)

Burgers may be eaten immediately since standing time is not needed.

Hamburger-Stuffed Squash

Preparation Time: 40 minutes
6 servings

Place in microwave oven:
2 whole acorn squash, pierced

Microwave on High for 10 minutes. Rearrange, then microwave at 50% for 5:00-7:00 (4:10-5:50) minutes. Combine in 2-quart casserole:
¾ lb. ground beef
¾ cup celery, chopped
3 Tbsp. onion, chopped

Microwave on High for 4:00-6:00 (3:20-5:00) minutes.

Stir in:
1 medium cooking apple, peeled, cored, and chopped (1 cup)

Microwave on High for 45 (38) seconds. Drain.

Combine and stir into beef mixture:
1 egg, slightly beaten
½ cup dairy sour cream

Cut squash in half; scoop out seeds; place cut side up and fill squash halves with beef mixture. Microwave on High for 5:00 (4:10) minutes. Sprinkle with:
¾ cup mild cheese, grated

Microwave at 50% for 60 (50) seconds to melt cheese. Serve hot.

Apple Ground Beef Stuffing

Preparation time: 18 minutes
4-6 servings

Combine in 3-quart casserole:
1 lb. ground beef
¼ cup onion, chopped
¼ cup celery, chopped
1 apple, pared and chopped

Microwave on High for 5:00-6:00 (4:10-5:00) minutes, or until vegetables are tender and beef is cooked.

Stir in:
1 cup water or apple juice

Microwave on High for 2:00 (1:40) minutes, or until juice is boiling. Stir in:
2 cups seasoned stuffing mix

Cover and let stand 5 minutes, or until moisture is absorbed. Fluff with a fork.

Note: Each recipe indicates two cooking times. The **first** is for a **650**-watt oven. The **second** (in parentheses) is for an **800**-watt oven.

Chinese Casserole

Preparation time: 14 minutes
6 servings

Combine in 1½-quart casserole:
1 can chicken noodle soup
1 can water
¾ cup quick cooking rice

Microwave 3-4 minutes. Let stand, covered.

Cook in 2-quart casserole on High for
5:00-6:00 (4:10-5:00) minutes:
1 lb. ground beef
1 large onion, sliced
½ cup green pepper, chopped
½ cup celery, chopped

Drain and stir in rice mixture. Cover and
microwave on High for 3:00-4:00
(2:30-3:20) minutes.

Ground Beef and Rice

Preparation Time: 23 minutes
6 servings

Microwave in 2-quart casserole for 5:00
(4:10) minutes.
1 lb. ground beef
1 small onion, chopped
¼ cup green pepper, chopped

Drain. Break up meat and stir in:
1 cup rice or macaroni, uncooked
2 cups spaghetti sauce (see page 70)
1 cup water
1 cup cheese, grated

Cover with casserole lid and microwave on
High to 150°F, about 12:00 (10:00) minutes.
Stir and microwave on High for 8:00-10:00
(6:40-8:20) minutes longer. You may need to
add more water if rice begins to dry out
before becoming tender.

Cabbage Rolls

Preparation time: 25 minutes
6 servings

In 2-quart glass measure microwave on
High for 5:00-6:00 (4:10-5:00) minutes, or
until boiling:
2 cups water

Immerse into boiling water:
**12 cabbage leaves, open side up, stem
side down**

Cover with plastic wrap and microwave on
High for 5:00 (4:10) minutes. Let stand
while mixing filling.

Combine:
1 lb. ground beef
2 potatoes, shredded
1 medium onion, chopped
½ cup celery, chopped

Note: Each recipe indicates two cooking times.
The **first** is for a **650**-watt oven.
The **second** (in parentheses) is for an **800**-watt oven.

1 tsp. salt
1 tsp. instant beef bouillon
1 tsp. prepared mustard
1 tsp. Worcestershire sauce
1/8 tsp. pepper
1 egg

Drain cabbage leaves. Place 1/3 cup meat filling at thin edge of leaf. Fold in sides. Roll up with filling inside. Place in glass baking dish with:
1/4 cup water

Cover with plastic wrap. Microwave on High for 12:00-13:00 (10:00-10:50) minutes.

Serve with tomato sauce or Seasoned White Sauce (below).

Seasoned White Sauce

Use Basic White Sauce (page 18) and stir in:
1/3 cup sour cream
1 tsp. chives

Top with paprika.

Creamed Dried Beef

Preparation Time: 10 minutes
2 servings

Combine in 1 1/2-quart casserole:
2 Tbsp. margarine
4 oz. dried beef, shredded

Microwave on High for 2:00 (1:40) minutes. Stir in:
2 Tbsp. flour

Microwave on High for 60 (50) seconds and gradually stir in:
1 cup warm milk

Microwave on High for 2:00 (1:40) minutes. Stir. Microwave on High another 2:00 (1:40) minutes.

Note: More cooking time may be necessary for a thicker sauce.

Hearty Onion Bake

Preparation Time: 20 minutes
6 servings

Microwave on High for 4:00-6:00
(3:20-5:00) minutes:
   ½ lb. pork sausage, removed from
   casing
   ½ lb. ground beef

Drain and divide between 6 1-cup
casseroles.

Combine and then divide between
casseroles:
   1 envelope onion soup mix
   1½ cups milk
   2 eggs, beaten

Microwave on High for 2:00-4:00
(1:40-3:20) minutes.

Top with:
   6 slices melba rounds
   6 slices tomato
   ¼ cup mild cheese, shredded

Microwave on High for 2:00-4:00
(1:40-3:20) minutes to melt cheese.
Serve warm.

Home-Prepared Spaghetti Sauce

Preparation Time: 10 minutes
Yields 4 cups

Microwave on High for 6:00-8:00
(5:00-6:40) minutes, or until internal
temperature of 150°F is reached:
   1 cup onion, chopped
   3 cups pureed tomatoes
   6-oz. can tomato paste
   1 tsp. basil
   1 Tbsp. oregano
   1 tsp. salt
   ¼ tsp. pepper

Note: Each recipe indicates two cooking times.
The **first** is for a **650**-watt oven.
The **second** (in parentheses) is for an **800**-watt oven.

PORK

Please see page 59 for guidelines on defrosting and cooking meats in the microwave.

Pork Roast

Place roast on roasting rack, fat side down.

Coat with browning agent, if desired.

Insert probe, being careful to avoid bone, fat, or air pockets.

Cover tightly with lid or plastic wrap, or place in cooking bag.

Shield with foil areas that have a tendency to brown too quickly.

Turn large pieces of meat over mid-way through cooking process to insure consistent doneness.

Roast at 30-70% to 160°F, testing at several places to be sure the correct temperature has been reached throughout.

Allow to stand 10 minutes.

Salt after cooking so the meat retains its moisture.

Carve and serve.

Pork Chops

Preparation Time: 10-15 minutes

For crisp cuts:

Use browning dish. Preheat 2:00-10:00 (1:40-8:20) minutes depending on size of browner and manufacturer's directions. Grease dish with butter or margarine for better color. Depending on size of piece of meat, microwave on High for 2:00-5:00 (1:40-4:10) minutes on each side.

Preparation Time: 5-10 minutes

For moister, more tender cuts:

Coat meat with favorite browning agent or seasoning (avoid salt). Place on meat rack. Cover with waxed paper. Microwave on High for 2:00-4:00 (1:40-3:20) minutes per piece. Turn over and repeat process.

Note: Each recipe indicates two cooking times.
The **first** is for a **650**-watt oven.
The **second** (in parentheses) is for an **800**-watt oven.

Fully Cooked Ham

Preparation Time: 5-8 minutes per pound

Most hams are fully cooked and only need to be warmed.

Place ham on roasting rack and cover to retain heat and moisture. Cook at 30-50% to an internal temperature of 120-130°F.

Bacon

Place paper towel on roasting rack or paper plate. Arrange bacon in single layer. Cover with paper towel. Microwave on High for about 60 (50) seconds per slice, or 15:00 (12:30) minutes per pound.

Note: See page 166 for Bacon Appetizers.

Apple Stuffed Tenderloin

Preparation Time: 25 minutes
4-6 servings

Combine in microwave-safe bowl:
2 Tbsp. butter
2 Tbsp. celery, chopped
2 Tbsp. onion, chopped

Microwave on High for 2:00 (1:40) minutes, or until vegetables are tender. Stir in:
1 1/2 cups stuffing mix
1/2 cup hot water

Slice lengthwise, three-quarters of the way through, then flatten and pound to even thickness:
1 1/2 pounds pork tenderloin

Fill with stuffing mixture and place on microwave roasting rack. Sprinkle with salt and pepper. Cover and microwave at 80% for 10:00 (8:20) minutes. Combine and spoon over meat:
1 envelope brown gravy mix
1/4 cup brown sugar
20-oz. can apple pie filling

Cover and microwave at 80% for 4:00-6:00 (2:30-5:00) minutes longer, or until meat reaches an internal temperature of 160°F.

Note: Each recipe indicates two cooking times.
The **first** is for a **650**-watt oven.
The **second** (in parentheses) is for an **800**-watt oven.

Pork and Rice a L'Orange

Preparation Time: 20 minutes
4 servings

Combine in 1½-quart glass baking dish:
   ½ cup minute rice
   ½ cup orange juice
   2 Tbsp. raisins
   1 Tbsp. water
   2 tsp. brown sugar
   ¼ tsp. salt
   ⅛ tsp. ground cinnamon

Mix well. Then arrange on top of rice mixture:
   1 pork tenderloin cut into 1 inch slices and seasoned with salt, pepper, and paprika

Cover with waxed paper and microwave on High for 9:00-10:00 (7:30-8:20) minutes, or until rice is tender and cutlets are done.

Pork Chop-Noodle Dinner

Preparation Time: 30 minutes
4 servings

Combine in glass baking dish:
   2 cups narrow noodles
   1 small onion, chopped
   1¼ cups water
   ⅓ cup catsup
   ½ tsp. salt
   ⅛ tsp. pepper

Arrange on top of noodles
   2 lbs. pork chops

Top with browning powder or paprika. Microwave on High for 22:00-25:00 (18:20-20:50) minutes, or until tender.

Note: Each recipe indicates two cooking times.
The **first** is for a **650**-watt oven.
The **second** (in parentheses) is for an **800**-watt oven.

Sweet and Sour Pork Kabobs

Preparation time: 25 minutes
4-6 servings

Combine in covered 1-quart casserole:
   6 carrots, peeled and cut into 1-inch
      pieces
   2 Tbsp. soy sauce

Microwave on High for 3:00-3:30
(2:30-2:55) minutes, or until steaming hot.

Add:
   1 lb. boneless pork, cut into 1-inch
      cubes

Cover. Microwave on High for 6:00-7:00
(5:00-5:50) minutes. Set aside.

Combine in 2-cup microwave-safe measure:
   juice from 8-oz. can of pineapple
      chunks
   2 Tbsp. sugar
   2 tsp. cornstarch
   1 Tbsp. soy sauce
   1 Tbsp. vinegar
   1 Tbsp. sweet pickle relish

Mix until smooth. Microwave uncovered on
High for 3:00-4:00 (2:30-3:20) minutes, or
until mixture boils and thickens, stirring
twice. Prepare:
   1 green pepper, cut into 1-inch pieces

Thread carrots, pineapple chunks, green
pepper, and pork alternately on 6-inch

bamboo skewers. Arrange on microwave-
safe platter and brush with sweet and sour
sauce. Cover with waxed paper. Microwave
on High for 3:00-4:00 (2:30-3:20) minutes.

Barbecued Ribs

Preparation Time: 30 minutes
4 servings

Arrange in glass baking dish:
   2 lbs. country-style ribs

Cover with waxed paper and microwave on
High for 7:00 (5:50) minutes. Turn over and
microwave on High another 7:00 (5:50)
minutes.

Combine and brush onto ribs:
   1 cup catsup
   ⅓ cup frozen concentrated
      lemonade
   3 Tbsp. brown sugar
   2 Tbsp. onion, chopped
   ¼ tsp. celery seed

Microwave on High for 11:00-12:00
(9:10-10:00) minutes, or until tender. The
ribs can also be roasted over hot coals at
this point.

Note: Each recipe indicates two cooking times.
The **first** is for a **650**-watt oven.
The **second** (in parentheses) is for an **800**-watt oven.

Orange-Glazed Ham Slices

Preparation time: 11 minutes
5 servings

Arrange on microwave-safe meat rack:
5 slices ham, about 1 pound

Cover with waxed paper. Microwave at 80%
for 4:00-5:00 (3:20-4:10) minutes.
Set aside.

Combine in microwave-safe 1-cup measure:
2 Tbsp. orange marmalade
1 Tbsp. dijon-style mustard
⅛ tsp. paprika

Microwave on High for 30-40 (25-35)
seconds, or until mixture bubbles.
Spoon over ham slices. Garnish
with orange slices and parsley.

Ham and Cheese Casserole

Preparation Time: 20 minutes
6-8 servings

Combine in 3-quart casserole dish:
8-oz. pkg. noodles, cooked
2 cups fully cooked ham, cut in
  pieces
1½ cups cheese, shredded
1 can cream of mushroom soup
1 cup frozen peas
½ tsp. dry mustard

Top with:
1 can fried onion rings

Cover with casserole lid and microwave at
80% for 12:00-15:00 (10:00-12:30) minutes.

Note: Each recipe indicates two cooking times.
The **first** is for a **650**-watt oven.
The **second** (in parentheses) is for an **800**-watt oven.

Pork Cassoulet

Preparation Time: 18 minutes
6-8 servings

Combine in microwaveable colander combination or 2-quart casserole:
1/2 lb. pork sausage, removed form casing
1 small onion, sliced
1 clove garlic, minced

Microwave on High for 2:00-4:00 (1:40-3:20) minutes, or until browned.

Turn into 2-quart casserole:
2 15-oz. cans navy beans with juice
1 1/2 cups fully cooked ham, cubed
1/4 cup dry white cooking wine, optional
2 Tbsp. parsley, snipped
1 bay leaf
dash of ground cloves

Microwave on High for 10:00-12:00 (8:20-10:00) minutes, stirring occasionally. Remove bay leaf. Serve in bowls.

Sausage and Apple Rings

Preparation time: 18 minutes
4 servings

Place in 1-quart baking dish:
2 medium apples, cored and sliced in 1/2-inch slices
1 cup cranberry juice cocktail

Microwave on High for 4:00-6:00 (3:20-5:00) minutes.

Combine while apples are cooking:
1 Tbsp. cornstarch
2 tsp. sugar
2 tsp. water

Remove apples from juice and stir in cornstarch mixture. Stir, then microwave on High for 3:00-4:00 (2:30-3:20) minutes, or until sauce thickens. Set aside.

Shape into 4 patties:
1 pound apple sausage

Dip into:
1 egg, beaten

Then dip into:
3/4 cup cracker crumbs, finely ground (about 20 saltines)

Brown on browning dish for 5:00-8:00 (4:10-6:40) minutes.

Top patties with apple slices and thickened sauce.

Sausage-Macaroni Skillet

Preparation Time: 25 minutes
6-8 servings

Combine in microwave-safe colander combination and microwave on High for 4:00-6:00 (3:20-5:00) minutes:
 1 lb. **Italian sausage, removed from casing**
 ½ cup **green peppers, chopped**
 ½ cup **onion, chopped**

Combine sausage mixture in 3-quart casserole with:
 16-oz. **can cut up tomatoes**
 10-oz. **can pizza sauce**
 ¼ tsp. **salt**

Microwave on High for 4:00-6:00 (3:20-5:00) minutes. Stir in:
 2 cups **zucchini, thinly sliced**

Microwave on High for 2:00-3:00 (1:40-2:30) minutes, or until zucchini is tender. Stir in:
 1 cup **dry medium-sized shell macaroni, cooked**

Sprinkle with:
 1 cup **mozzarella cheese, shredded**

Microwave on High for 2:00-3:00 (1:40-2:30) minutes, until cheese is melted and macaroni mixture is warm.

Rice and Sausage Casserole

Preparation Time: 20 minutes
6 servings

Microwave on High for 4:00-6:00 (3:20-5:00) minutes in microwavable colander combination or 2-quart casserole:
 1 lb. **pork sausage, removed from casing**
 1 small **onion, finely chopped**

Drain, then layer in 2-quart casserole with sausage mixture:
 3 cups **rice, cooked**

Pour on:
 1 can **condensed tomato, celery, mushroom, or chicken soup**

Sprinkle over top:
 ¼ cup **cheddar cheese, shredded**

Cover and microwave on High 6:00-8:00 (5:00-6:40) minutes.

Note: Each recipe indicates two cooking times.
The **first** is for a **650**-watt oven.
The **second** (in parentheses) is for an **800**-watt oven.

Night-Before Sausage Brunch

Preparation Time: 35 minutes
6-8 servings

Layer in 9 x 13 greased microwave-safe baking dish:
12 link sausages, cooked
12 slices bread, buttered and cubed
1 cup cheese, shredded

Mix and pour over bread and sausage:
8 eggs
4 cups milk

Cover with a thick layer of:
cornflake crumbs, crushed

Cover, refrigerate overnight, then microwave at 50% for 25:00-35:00 (20:50-29:10) minutes, or until set in the center.

Sausage Panwiches

Preparation Time: 4 minutes
1 serving

Spread:
2 Tbsp. apple butter

On:
2 cooked pancakes

Set aside.

Crumble into 1-quart glass microwave-safe dish:
¼ cup loose sausage, cooked, or
1 link pre-cooked sausage

Microwave on High for 2:00 (1:40) minutes. Sprinkle over pancakes. Microwave on High for 30-45 (25-38) seconds.

Hot Dogs

Place regular-sized hot dog in bun. Wrap in paper towel and microwave on High for 30-50 (25-42) seconds.

Note: Each recipe indicates two cooking times. The **first** is for a **650**-watt oven. The **second** (in parentheses) is for an **800**-watt oven.

Stuffed Hot Dogs

Preparation Time: 10 minutes
4 servings

Microwave between paper towels on High
for 2:00-3:00 (1:40-2:30) minutes:
   4 slices bacon

Slit:
   4 hot dogs

Stuff with:
   4 slices cheese
   mustard
   relish

Wrap with partially cooked bacon. Secure
with wooden picks. Microwave between
paper towels on High for 2:00-3:00
(1:40-2:30) minutes. Remove wooden picks
and serve in warm rolls.

Hot Dogs and Sauerkraut

Preparation Time: 15 minutes
8 servings

Combine in 2-quart casserole:
   1 pkg. brown gravy mix
   ¼ cup brown sugar
   ½ cup beer or apple juice
   1 lb. sauerkraut
   1 small onion, sliced

Mix in:
   1 lb. hot dogs, scored

Cover with lid. Microwave on High for
8:00-10:00 (6:40-8:20) minutes, or to 135°F.

*Note: Wursts or other meats can be
substituted for hot dogs.*

Hot Dogs and Baked Beans

Preparation Time: 9 minutes
4 servings

Arrange 4 hot dogs in casserole. Cover with
16-oz. can of baked beans. Microwave at
80% for 6:00-8:00 (5:00-6:40) minutes.

Note: Each recipe indicates two cooking times.
The **first** is for a **650**-watt oven.
The **second** (in parentheses) is for an **800**-watt oven.

POULTRY

Quick Cooking Creates Moist, Tender Meat

- Defrost at 30% for 7:00-8:00 (5:50-6:40) minutes per pound. Make sure meat is completely defrosted before beginning to cook it.

- Whenever possible remove the skin from the bird before microwaving it. Because of its high fat content the skin retains moisture and, thus, never gets crisp; it even prevents proper cooking of the meat itself.

- Cover the bird to retain moisture while cooking. The tighter the cover, the more moist the meat. Plastic wrap, a cooking bag, or a tightly fitting casserole lid all work well.

- Microwave poultry on a rack to elevate it above its hot juices, which may overcook its underside.

- Microwave at 70% for 7:30 (6:15) minutes per pound. Whole birds up to 14 pounds can be microwaved.

- Stuffing does not increase the per-pound cooking time.

- Use aluminum foil to cover portions that may seem to be cooking too quickly, like the wings or drumsticks.

- Turn bird over mid-way through cooking time.

- Be sure there is enough room around the bird in your oven—at least one inch on all sides—to allow for the proper circulation of air and microwaves.

- Standing time is essential to assure that the roasted bird is fully cooked. Allow 7-10 minutes.

Chicken Breasts

For maximum crispness remove skin and coat with Crisp Crumb Mixture (right).

Arrange on roasting rack, with the thickest part of the meat toward the outside.

Cover with waxed paper or plastic wrap.

Microwave at 70% for 7:30 (6:15) minutes per pound (whole breasts weigh close to a pound).

Chicken Pieces

Coat with Crisp Crumb Mixture or chicken-coating mix.

Arrange on meat rack with thicker portions to the outside.

Cover with plastic wrap or waxed paper.

Microwave at 70% for 7:30 (6:15) minutes per pound.

Crisp Crumb Mixture

Combine:
1/2 cup dry bread crumbs
1/2 cup Parmesan cheese
1/2 tsp. paprika
dash pepper

Soy Chicken

Preparation Time: 25 minutes
6 8 servings

Place in cooking bag, then put in glass baking dish:
2 1/2-lb. chicken, stuffed with
1 small onion

Combine and pour over chicken:
1/4 cup soy sauce
1/4 cup orange juice
1/4 tsp. ground ginger

Seal bag. Pierce. Microwave at 70% for 18:00-20:00 (15:00-16:40) minutes.

Note: Each recipe indicates two cooking times.
The **first** is for a **650**-watt oven.
The **second** (in parentheses) is for an **800**-watt oven.

Barbecued Chicken

Microwave chicken pieces at 70% for 3:30 (2:55) minutes per pound.

Brush with Barbecue Sauce (below).

Turn pieces over and brush with Sauce.

Microwave at 70% for another 3:30 (2:55) minutes per pound, or roast over hot coals.

Barbecue Sauce

Combine and mix well:
  1 cup catsup
  1/3 cup frozen concentrated lemonade
  3 Tbsp. brown sugar
  2 Tbsp. onion, chopped
  1/4 tsp. celery seed

Sweet and Sour Chicken

Preparation Time: 20 minutes
4 servings

Combine in pie plate:
  3 Tbsp. flour
  1/2 cup brown sugar
  1/4 tsp. salt

Cut into 1/2-inch cubes:
  1 1/2 lbs. chicken

Coat with flour mixture and arrange in baking pan. Combine and pour over chicken:
  1/4 cup soy sauce
  1/3 cup vinegar
  1/4 cup water

Top with:
  1 onion, sliced
  1 pepper, sliced

Microwave on High for 6:00 (5:00) minutes. Stir. Microwave on High for 6:00 (5:00) more minutes.

Note: Each recipe indicates two cooking times. The **first** is for a **650**-watt oven. The **second** (in parentheses) is for an **800**-watt oven.

Chicken Parmesan

Preparation Time: 20 minutes
4 servings

Combine in pie plate:
2 Tbsp. flour
1/2 tsp. salt
dash pepper

Dredge in flour mixture:
4 boneless chicken breast halves

Dip in egg wash mixture of:
1 egg
2 Tbsp. milk or water

Dip in:
Crisp Crumb Mixture (page 82)

Brown in browning dish.

Layer in small casserole dish:
1/2 cup spaghetti sauce (see page 70)
breaded and browned chicken breasts
1/4 cup Parmesan cheese
1/4 cup mozzarella cheese, grated

Microwave on High for 4:00-6:00
(3:20-5:00) minutes, until cheese is melted
and sauce is bubbling.

Cordon Bleu

Preparation Time: 25 minutes
4 servings

Pound until even thickness:
4 boneless chicken breast halves

Layer on top of each piece of chicken:
1 slice cooked ham (4 slices total)
1 slice Gruyere cheese (4 slices total)

Roll up each breast and dip in:
4 Tbsp. butter, melted

Roll in:
cracker crumbs, crushed

Position in baking pan on top of Stuffing
(see page 43). Cover with waxed paper.
Microwave at 80% for 15:00 (12:30)
minutes.

Note: Each recipe indicates two cooking times.
The **first** is for a **650**-watt oven.
The **second** (in parentheses) is for an **800**-watt oven.

Chicken Kiev

Preparation Time: 25 minutes
4 servings

Pound until even thickness:
4 boneless chicken breast halves

Stuff each piece of chicken with:
1 Tbsp. butter, frozen (4 Tbsp. total)
salt
pepper
chives

Tuck in sides and roll up.

Dip each roll in:
cracker crumbs, crushed,
**   or coating mix**

Position in baking pan on top of Stuffing (see page 43). Cover with waxed paper. Microwave at 80% for 15:00 (12:30) minutes.

Roast Turkey

Preparation Time, after defrosting: 1½ hours
About 10 servings

To defrost a:
12-lb. frozen turkey

Microwave at 30% for 45:00 (37:30) minutes.

Place thawed turkey in nylon cooking bag and lay in large baking dish. Roast at 70% for 45:00 (37:30) minutes. Turn turkey over. Roast at 70% for another 45:00 (37:30) minutes.

Reserve cooking juices for Gravy (see page 86).

Note: Each recipe indicates two cooking times. The **first** is for a **650**-watt oven. The **second** (in parentheses) is for an **800**-watt oven.

Gravy from Roast Turkey

Preparation Time: 6-8 minutes
Yields 1½ cups gravy

In four-cup microwave-safe glass measure mix until lump-free:
  2 Tbsp. flour
  ¼ cup water

Add, stirring until smooth:
  1 cup broth from Roast Turkey
  (see page 85)

Microwave on High for 2:00 (1:40) minutes. Stir. Microwave on High another 2:00 (1:40) minutes. Stir. Continue until Gravy reaches desired consistency.

Chicken and Rice

Preparation Time: 27 minutes
6 servings

Combine in 5-quart casserole or 9 x 13 glass dish:
  1½ cups rice, uncooked
  1 can cream of mushroom, celery, or chicken soup
  4-oz. can mushrooms
  1½ cups water

Top with:
  3 lbs. chicken pieces

Cover with lid or plastic wrap. Microwave on High for 10:00 (8:20) minutes. Rotate pan. Microwave on High for 10:00-12:00 (8:20-10:00) more minutes, or until rice is tender and chicken is done.

Note: Each recipe indicates two cooking times.
The **first** is for a **650**-watt oven.
The **second** (in parentheses) is for an **800**-watt oven.

Chicken-Rice Bake

Preparation Time: 35 minutes
4-6 servings

Place on paper plate between paper towels:
3 slices bacon

Microwave on High for 3:00 (2:30) minutes, or until crisp.

Set aside.

Combine in 12 x 8 glass baking dish:
3/4 cup rice
1 cup chicken broth
1 can condensed cream soup

Cover with waxed paper. Microwave on High for 6:00-7:00 (5:00-5:50) minutes. Stir in:
bacon, crumbled

Top with:
2-3 lbs. frying chicken, cut in pieces

Sprinkle with browning powder or paprika. Microwave at 70% for 15:00-23:00 (12:30-19:10) minutes.

Chicken a la King

Preparation Time: 12 minutes
2-4 servings

Combine in 1½-quart microwave-safe casserole:
2 Tbsp. margarine
4 oz. chicken, cubed and cooked

Microwave on High for 2:00 (1:40) minutes. Stir in:
2 Tbsp. flour

Microwave on High for 60 (50) seconds; then gradually stir in:
1 cup warm milk
½ cup mixed vegetables

Microwave on High for 3:00 (2:30) minutes. Stir, then serve in pastry shells or over rice.

Note: This is a handy way to use leftover chicken and vegetables.

Note: Each recipe indicates two cooking times.
The **first** is for a **650**-watt oven.
The **second** (in parentheses) is for an **800**-watt oven.

Notes

Note: Each recipe indicates two cooking times.
The **first** is for a **650**-watt oven.
The **second** (in parentheses) is for an **800**-watt oven.

VEAL

Please see page 59 for guidelines on defrosting and cooking meats in the microwave.

Veal Cutlets

Preparation Time: 20 minutes
3-4 servings

Combine in pie plate:
2 Tbsp. flour
1/2 tsp. salt
dash pepper

Work flour mixture into:
2 veal cutlets

Preheat browning dish and add:
4 Tbsp. butter
1 onion, sliced

Add cutlets. Microwave on High for 3:00 (2:30) minutes. Turn. Microwave on High another 3:00 (2:30) minutes. Cover. Microwave at 30% for 2:00-3:00 (1:40-2:30) more minutes, or until the meat is tender.

Veal Scallopini

Preparation Time: 20 minutes
4 servings

Combine:
1 Tbsp. flour
1/2 tsp. salt
dash pepper

Dredge in flour mixture:
1 lb. veal, thinly sliced

Microwave on High for 2:00 (1:40) minutes to heat, then add meat to:
1/4 cup salad oil

Add:
1/2 onion, sliced

Microwave on High for 4:00-6:00 (3:20-5:00) minutes, or until tender, then add:
16-oz. can tomatoes, cut up and | drained
3-oz. can sliced mushrooms, drained
1 Tbsp. fresh parsley
1/4 tsp. garlic salt
1/4 tsp. dried oregano

Cook on High for 5:00-6:00 (4:10-5:00) minutes, or until heated through. Serve over hot buttered noodles.

Note: Each recipe indicates two cooking times.
The **first** is for a **650**-watt oven.
The **second** (in parentheses) is for an **800**-watt oven.

Veal Scallops and Spaghetti

Preparation Time: 25 minutes
3 servings

Microwave 6 cups water on High for 10:00-12:00 (8:20-10:00) minutes, or until boiling.

Add:
6-oz. spaghetti

Cover and microwave on High for 12:00-14:00 (10:00-11:40) minutes.

Drain and rinse in cold water. Set aside.

Combine in 2-cup glass measure:
1 cup fresh mushrooms, sliced
1 small onion, sliced
1 clover garlic, minced
1 Tbsp. margarine

Microwave uncovered on High for 3:00-4:00 (2:30-3:20) minutes, or until tender, stirring once.

Mix in:
1/2 tsp. salt
1/4 tsp. dried oregano
8-oz. can tomato sauce

Set aside.

Pound with meat mallet until very thin:
8 oz. veal scallops or cutlets

Sprinkle both sides with:
**natural meat browning and
   seasoning powder**

Cut into half-inch strips. Place in 1-quart glass casserole. Pour sauce over meat.

Microwave uncovered on High for 7:00-8:00 (5:50-6:40) minutes, or until veal is tender.

Place spaghetti on glass serving plate. Spoon meat and sauce over spaghetti.

Microwave on High for 1:30-2:00 (1:15-1:40) minutes, or until heated through.

Veal Tenderloin

Preparation Time: 15 minutes
3-4 servings

Combine in 1-cup microwave-safe measuring cup:
**1/3 cup pineapple juice (reserve
   pineapple chunks)**
2 Tbsp. brown sugar
1 tsp. cornstarch
1/8 tsp. dry mustard
dash ground cloves
1/8 tsp. paprika

Blend until smooth. Microwave uncovered on High for 1:00-1:30 (50 seconds-1:15 minutes) minutes, or until mixture boils. Set aside.

Place in microwave-safe dish:
3/4 lb. veal tenderloin

Brush with sauce. Cover. Cook at 80% for 8:00 (6:40) minutes, or until internal temperature reaches 130°F. Slice and serve with pineapples and remaining sauce.

Note: Each recipe indicates two cooking times. The **first** is for a **650**-watt oven. The **second** (in parentheses) is for an **800**-watt oven.

Notes

Note: Each recipe indicates two cooking times.
The **first** is for a **650**-watt oven.
The **second** (in parentheses) is for an **800**-watt oven.

FISH AND SEAFOOD

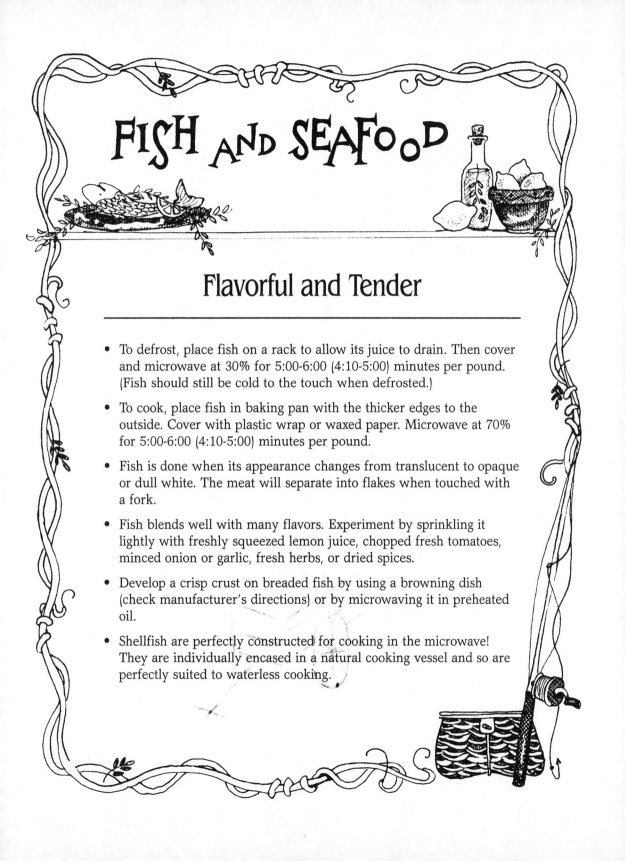

Flavorful and Tender

- To defrost, place fish on a rack to allow its juice to drain. Then cover and microwave at 30% for 5:00-6:00 (4:10-5:00) minutes per pound. (Fish should still be cold to the touch when defrosted.)

- To cook, place fish in baking pan with the thicker edges to the outside. Cover with plastic wrap or waxed paper. Microwave at 70% for 5:00-6:00 (4:10-5:00) minutes per pound.

- Fish is done when its appearance changes from translucent to opaque or dull white. The meat will separate into flakes when touched with a fork.

- Fish blends well with many flavors. Experiment by sprinkling it lightly with freshly squeezed lemon juice, chopped fresh tomatoes, minced onion or garlic, fresh herbs, or dried spices.

- Develop a crisp crust on breaded fish by using a browning dish (check manufacturer's directions) or by microwaving it in preheated oil.

- Shellfish are perfectly constructed for cooking in the microwave! They are individually encased in a natural cooking vessel and so are perfectly suited to waterless cooking.

- Place shellfish on paper plate and microwave at 70% until done:
  - Clams are done when their shells open—about 2:00 (1:40) minutes per dozen.
  - Crabs are done when their shells turn pink. The cooking time varies considerably depending on the size of the crab, so watch carefully.
  - Lobster is done when its shell turns red. That may take from 4:00 (3:20) to 10:00 (8:20) minutes, depending upon its size.
  - Oysters are done when their shells open—about 2:00-5:00 (1:40-4:10) minutes per dozen.
  - Shrimp are done when their shells turn pink—about 60 (50) seconds per dozen, again, depending on their size.

Fresh Catch

Preparation Time: 12 minutes
4 servings

Arrange in glass baking dish with thicker portions toward outside of dish:
2-3 small cleaned fish, or 1-lb. fillet
1 small onion, sliced
1/2 lemon, squeezed
salt and pepper

Cover with plastic wrap and microwave at 70% for 5:00-8:00 (4:10-6:40) minutes, or until fish looks opaque and flakes with a fork.

Fish in Wine Sauce

Preparation Time: 10 minutes
4 servings

Arrange in 8-inch square baking dish with thicker portions to the outside:
1 lb. fish fillets

Cover with waxed paper. Microwave at 70% for 5:00-8:00 (4:10-6:40) minutes, or until fish is opaque and flakes.

Combine in 1-cup glass measure and microwave on High for 60 (50) seconds, then stir to combine:

1 Tbsp. butter
2 Tbsp. lemon juice
2 Tbsp. cooking wine
1/2 tsp. salt

Arrange fillets on serving dish. Drizzle with sauce and garnish with:
paprika, lemon slices, parsley

Yogurt Fillets

Preparation Time: 8 minutes
About 4 servings

Arrange in 8-inch round glass baking dish:
14-16 ozs. haddock or other fish
fillets

Cover with plastic wrap.

Microwave on High for 4:00-4:30 (3:20-3:45) minutes, or until fish flakes apart easily with fork.

Combine for sauce:
1/3 cup plain yogurt
1/2 tsp. salt
1 tsp. prepared mustard
1 tsp. chopped pimento
1 tsp. fresh parsley
1 tsp. lemon juice

Drain fish. Spoon sauce over fish.

Microwave on High for 1:00-1:30 (50 seconds-1:15 minutes) minutes, or until sauce is heated through.

Note: Each recipe indicates two cooking times. The **first** is for a **650**-watt oven. The **second** (in parentheses) is for an **800**-watt oven.

Crunchy Fillets

Preparation Time: 7 minutes
About 2 servings

Place in shallow 1½-quart glass baking
dish:
   2 Tbsp. butter or margarine

Microwave on High for 30-60 (25-50)
seconds, or until melted.

Arrange in butter:
   8-ozs. fish fillets

Turn to coat both sides.

Combine:
   2 Tbsp. almonds, finely chopped
   2 Tbsp. wheat germ
   1 Tbsp. Parmesan cheese
   ¼ tsp. salt

Spoon onto fillets. Cover with paper towel.

Microwave on High for 2:30-3:30
(2:05-2:55) minutes, or until fish flakes apart
easily with fork.

Note: For a double recipe, increase final
microwave time to 4:00-5:00 (3:20-4:10)
minutes. If desired, toast almonds before
adding by placing in glass pie plate and
microwaving on High for 4:00-5:00 (3:20-4:10)
minutes. Stir every minute.

Stuffed Trout

Preparation Time: 20 minutes
3 servings

Combine in glass mixing bowl:
   3 Tbsp. butter or margarine
   ½ cup celery, chopped
   2 Tbsp. onion, chopped

Microwave uncovered on High for
4:00-4:30 (3:20-3:45) minutes, or until
vegetables are tender.

Stir in:
   3 slices bread, cubed
   1 tsp. dried parsley flakes

Rinse and pat dry:
   1 whole trout (about 16 ounces)

Sprinkle cavity with:
   ½ tsp. salt

Place on glass serving plate. Spoon stuffing
mixture into cavity, letting excess stuffing
overflow.

Place on stuffing inside cavity:
   2-3 slices lemon

Cover with plastic wrap.

Microwave on High for 6:00-7:00
(5:00-5:50) minutes, or until fish flakes apart
easily with fork, rotating plate once. Let
stand covered a few minutes before serving.
If desired, garnish with additional lemon
slices and parsley.

Note: Each recipe indicates two cooking times.
The **first** is for a **650**-watt oven.
The **second** (in parentheses) is for an **800**-watt oven.

Note: Stuffing can be prepared ahead and inserted just before cooking. Lemon slices can be omitted. Add 1 Tbsp. lemon juice to stuffing, if desired.

Sole Florentine

Preparation Time: 20 minutes
About 4 servings

In microwave-safe container, microwave on High for 5:00-6:00 (4:10-5:00) minutes, or until thawed:
1 pkg. (10 ozs.) frozen chopped spinach

Drain. Arrange in 8-inch round glass baking dish.

Arrange on top of spinach:
12-16 ozs. sole or other fish fillets

Set aside.

Combine:
1 cup milk
2 Tbsp. flour
1 tsp. salt
1/2 tsp. tarragon leaves

Mix well.

Add:
2 Tbsp. butter or margarine

Microwave uncovered on High for 3:00-4:00 (2:30-3:20) minutes, or until mixture boils and thickens, stirring twice during last half of cooking time.

Stir in:
1 Tbsp. lemon juice

Pour over fillets.

Sprinkle with:
1/4 cup Parmesan cheese
paprika

Cover with waxed paper.

Microwave on High for 5:00-6:00 (4:10-5:00) minutes, or until fish flakes apart easily with fork, rotating dish once.

Note: The spinach can be thawed and sauce prepared several hours ahead. Assemble with fish just before cooking and serving.

Fish Fillets with Mushrooms

Preparation Time: 10 minutes
3-4 servings

Arrange in 12 x 7 inch baking dish:
1 lb. fish fillets

Combine and pour over fish:
1 tsp. lemon juice
2 Tbsp. water

Top with:
2 green onions, thinly sliced
1/2 cup mushrooms, sliced
1 tomato, peeled and cubed

Cover with waxed paper. Microwave at 70% for 5:00-7:00 (4:10-5:50) minutes.

Note: Each recipe indicates two cooking times. The **first** is for a **650**-watt oven. The **second** (in parentheses) is for an **800**-watt oven.

Shrimp in a Dish

Preparation Time: 10 minutes
4 servings

Arrange in 9-inch glass pie plate:
1 lb. shrimp, peeled

Combine in glass measure and pour over shrimp:
2 Tbsp. cooking sherry
1 clove garlic, pressed
dash red pepper sauce
juice from ½ lemon

Top shrimp with:
6 butter crackers, crushed into crisp crumbs

Cover with waxed paper. Microwave on high for 4:00-6:00 (3:20-5:00) minutes. Serve with lemon wedges.

Oriental Shrimp

Preparation Time: 20 minutes
4-5 servings

Combine in 1½-quart glass casserole:
¼ cup butter or margarine
2 cups fresh mushrooms, sliced
1¼ cup green onions, sliced
1 clove garlic, minced

Microwave uncovered on High for 2:00-3:00 (1:40-2:30) minutes, or until nearly tender.

Stir in:
1 Tbsp. arrowroot,
**   or 2 Tbsp. cornstarch**
2 Tbsp. soy sauce
½ tsp. salt
12 ozs. frozen uncooked shrimp

Cover with casserole lid.

Microwave on High for 5:00-6:00 (4:10-5:00) minutes, or until shrimp are no longer icy, stirring once.

Run warm water over, until separated:
1 pkg. (6 ounces) frozen pea pods

Stir in pea pods and:
1 cup fresh bean sprouts

Cover.

Microwave on High for 6:00-7:00 (5:00-5:50) minutes, or until vegetables are tender and shrimp are firm, stirring once or twice. Serve alone or over rice.

Note: Each recipe indicates two cooking times.
The **first** is for a **650**-watt oven.
The **second** (in parentheses) is for an **800**-watt oven.

Individual Salmon Loaves

Preparation Time: 25 minutes
4-5 servings

Combine in mixing bowl:
   15½-oz. can salmon, drained
   1 egg

Mix with fork.

Stir in:
   1 cup soft bread crumbs
   ⅓ cup milk
   2 Tbsp. onion, finely chopped
   1 Tbsp. lemon juice
   ¼ tsp. salt
   dash pepper

Mix well. Spoon evenly into four or five 5-oz. glass custard cups and press firmly. Place cups on glass plate or tray for ease in transferring to oven. Cover with waxed paper.

Microwave on High for 5:30-6:00 (4:35-5:00) minutes, or until centers of loaves are set, rotating plate once. Let stand covered and set aside.

Microwave in microwave-safe container on High for 5:00-6:00 (4:10-5:00) minutes, or until tender:
   1 pkg. (10 ozs.) asparagus pieces or spears

Set aside.

Beat together with fork in 1-cup glass measure:
   ½ cup mayonnaise
   1 egg

Mix in:
   1 Tbsp. lemon juice
   ¼ tsp. tarragon leaves
   ¼ tsp. prepared mustard

Microwave uncovered at 50% for 1:15-1:30 (1:12-1:25) minutes, or until slightly thickened, stirring twice.

Unmold salmon onto serving plate. Arrange asparagus in center of or around salmon. Spoon sauce over salmon and asparagus.

Microwave uncovered on High for 1:00-2:00 (50 seconds-1:40) minutes, or until heated through.

Note: Salmon loaves can be made ahead and refrigerated 1-2 days. Increase first microwave time to 7:00-7:30 (5:50-6:15) minutes. If cooking only half the loaves, decrease time to 3:00-4:00 (2:30-3:20) minutes.

Note: Each recipe indicates two cooking times. The **first** is for a **650**-watt oven. The **second** (in parentheses) is for an **800**-watt oven.

Coquilles St. Jacques (Scallops in Cream Sauce)

Preparation Time: 15 minutes
4-6 servings

In 2-quart microwave-safe casserole combine:
½ cup butter
1 Tbsp. onion, minced

Microwave uncovered on High for 2:00 (1:40) minutes. Stir in:
2 Tbsp. flour

Add, blending well:
4 ozs. mushrooms, sliced
¼ cup dry vermouth, or apple juice
½ tsp. salt
⅛ tsp. white pepper
1 lb. bay scallops
1 bay leaf
2 tsp. lemon juice

Stir carefully, cover, and microwave on High for 6:00 (5:00) minutes, or until scallops are tender. Remove bay leaf. Whisk together:
½ cup light cream
1 egg yolk

Gradually whisk some of the hot mixture into the egg and cream. When smooth, add that to the remaining sauce. Cover and microwave at 50% for 5:00 (4:10) minutes.

Watch carefully, and if the sauce begins to boil, stir immediately to avoid curdling or separation. If this condition does occur, more cream can be added to bring sauce back to normal consistency.

Seafood Newburg

Preparation Time: 15 minutes
4-6 servings

Substitute 1 lb. of any seafood for the scallops in the Coquilles St. Jacques recipe above.

Serve on patty shells.

Seafood Splash

Preparation Time: 17 minutes
4-5 servings

Partially thaw:
1 pkg. (6 ozs.) frozen crabmeat and shrimp

Combine in 1½-quart casserole:
2 cups shredded potatoes, or 12 ozs. frozen hash brown potatoes, thawed
1 Tbsp. butter or margarine
2 green onions, sliced (including tops)

Cover with casserole lid.

Note: Each recipe indicates two cooking times.
The **first** is for a **650**-watt oven.
The **second** (in parentheses) is for an **800**-watt oven.

Microwave on High for 4:30-5:30 (3:45-4:35) minutes, or until potatoes are almost tender, stirring once.

Stir in:
10¾-oz. can condensed cream of celery soup
¾ cup sour cream
1 Tbsp. lemon juice
¼ tsp. garlic salt

Add seafood. Cover.

Microwave on High for 4:00-5:00 (3:20-4:10) minutes, or until hot. Stir well.

Sprinkle with:
½ cup cheddar cheese, shredded
2 Tbsp. sliced green olives, if desired
paprika

Microwave uncovered on High for 2:00-2:30 (1:40-2:05) minutes, or until cheese is melted.

Seafood Casserole

Preparation Time: 15 minutes
4 servings

Combine in 1½-quart casserole, then cover with casserole lid and microwave on High for 3:00 (2:30) minutes:
3 Tbsp. green onions, sliced
½ cup celery, chopped

Stir in:
2 cans cream of mushroom soup
8 ozs. small shrimp, peeled
6 ozs. crabmeat
½ cup cashews
2 cups chow mein noodles

Microwave on High for 3:00 (2:30) minutes. Stir. Microwave on High for 2:00-3:00 (1:40-2:30) minutes more.

Fish Medley

Preparation Time: 15
3 servings

Cut into matchstick pieces:
2 carrots
2 potatoes

Place in 1-quart casserole with:
2 Tbsp. water

Cover and microwave on High for 7:00-8:00 (5:50-6:40) minutes. Season and set aside.

Cut into serving-size pieces and arrange in 2-quart casserole over vegetables:
12 ozs. fish

Add:
3 Tbsp. white wine or lemon juice
½ lemon, sliced
½ tsp. salt
dash pepper

Microwave on High for 4:00 (3:20) minutes, or until fish flakes.

Note: Each recipe indicates two cooking times. The **first** is for a **650**-watt oven. The **second** (in parentheses) is for an **800**-watt oven.

Fish Creole

Preparation Time: 25 minutes
6 servings

Combine in 2-quart casserole, then
microwave on High for 4:00 (3:20) minutes:
  1 green pepper, sliced
  1 1/2 cups green onions, sliced
  2 Tbsp. butter

Stir in:
  2 cups tomatoes, cut up and drained
  1 cup tomato sauce
  1/2 tsp. ground thyme
  1 bay leaf
  salt and pepper

Arrange on top of sauce:
  1 1/2 lbs. flounder fillets

Cover with waxed paper. Microwave
on High for 8:00 (6:40) minutes. Let stand
5 minutes. Serve over cooked rice.

Bouillabaisse

Preparation Time: 30 minutes
5-6 servings

Combine in 2-quart glass casserole:
  1 medium onion, chopped
  1 clove garlic, minced
  1 Tbsp. vegetable oil

Microwave uncovered on High for
3:00-4:00 (2:30-3:20) minutes, or until
tender, stirring once.

Stir in:
  28-oz. can whole tomatoes,
    undrained
  1 bay leaf
  1 tsp. instant chicken bouillon
  1/2 tsp. salt
  1/2 tsp. thyme leaves
  1/8 tsp. ground allspice, if desired
  6 drops Tabasco sauce

Microwave uncovered on High for
13:00-15:00 (10:50-12:30) minutes, or until
flavors are blended, stirring once.

Cut into 1-inch pieces:
  1 lb. fish fillets (red snapper, turbot,
    or pike)

To tomato mixture add fish and:
  6 ozs. frozen uncooked shrimp

Cover.

Microwave on High for 7:00-7:30
(5:50-6:15) minutes, or until fish flakes apart
easily and shrimp are firm, stirring twice.

Note: Each recipe indicates two cooking times.
The **first** is for a **650**-watt oven.
The **second** (in parentheses) is for an **800**-watt oven.

Remove bay leaf. Garnish with parsley and lemon slices.

Note: Crab, lobster, or clams can be combined with fish. Frozen cooked shrimp can be substituted for uncooked shrimp. Timings will be very similar.

Fish and Broccoli Bake

Preparation Time: 30 minutes
4-5 servings

In microwave-safe container, microwave on High for 4:00-4:30 (3:20-3:45) minutes, or until nearly tender:
1 pkg. (10 ozs.) frozen chopped broccoli

Drain and set aside.

Combine in 1½-qt. glass casserole:
¼ cup butter or margarine
½ cup celery, chopped
2 Tbsp. onion, chopped

Cover with casserole lid.

Microwave on High for 4:00-4:30 (3:20-3:45) minutes, or until vegetables are almost tender. Stir in:
2 Tbsp. flour
½ tsp. salt
½ cup milk
3 Tbsp. dry cooking sherry (optional; see Note below)

Microwave on High for 3:00-4:00 (2:30-3:20) minutes, or until mixture boils and thickens, stirring once or twice.

Stir in drained broccoli and:
½ cup (2 ozs.) cheddar cheese, shredded

Cut into 1-inch pieces:
14-16 ozs. fish fillets (turbot, snapper, or halibut)

Add to broccoli mixture. Cover.

Microwave on High for 3:30-4:00 (2:55-3:20) minutes, stirring once.

Top with:
½ cup (2 ozs.) cheddar cheese, shredded

Microwave on High for 2:00-2:30 (1:40-2:05) minutes, or until fish flakes apart easily with fork and mixture is bubbly.

Note: Frozen mixed vegetables can be substituted for broccoli. Sherry can be omitted; then increase milk to ⅔ cup.

Note: Each recipe indicates two cooking times.
The **first** is for a **650**-watt oven.
The **second** (in parentheses) is for an **800**-watt oven.

Hot Tuna Sandwiches

Preparation Time: 7 minutes
6-8 servings

Combine in small mixing bowl:
9 1/2-oz. can tuna, drained
1/2 cup celery, chopped
1/4 cup green onions, sliced
**1 cup (4 ozs.) Swiss or cheddar
cheese, shredded**
3 hard-cooked eggs, chopped
1/3 cup mayonnaise
1/3 cup sour cream
2 Tbsp. chopped pimento, drained
1 1/2 tsp. lemon juice

Mix well.

Cut in half lengthwise:
**1 small loaf French bread (about
12 inches long)**

Scoop out center of bread leaving a 12-inch shell. Place crust-side down on glass serving plate. Fill each half with tuna mixture and garnish with parsley. Microwave uncovered on High for 2:00-2:30 (1:40-2:05) minutes, or until heated, rotating plate once. Cut into 6-8 sections.

Note: The bread that is removed can be used for bread crumbs. Individual sandwiches can be made by using French rolls. To make fewer than six sandwiches, fill the number of rolls desired and refrigerate remaining filling. Microwave smaller quantity on High for 20-30 (17-25) seconds for each sandwich.

Jiffy Tuna Casserole

Preparation Time: 20 minutes
About 6 servings

Combine in 1 1/2-quart, microwave-safe casserole:
**10 3/4-oz. can condensed mushroom
soup**
**6 1/2-oz. can water-packed light tuna,
drained**
2-oz. can sliced mushrooms, undrained
**4 ozs. uncooked egg noodles
(about 2 cups)**
1 1/3 cups milk
1 cup frozen peas
1/8 tsp. pepper

Cover with casserole lid. Microwave on High for 12:00-14:00 (10:00-11:40) minutes, or until noodles are tender and sauce is creamy, stirring twice. Let stand covered for 5 minutes.

Sprinkle with:
1 3/4-oz. can shoestring potatoes

Note: Peas can be omitted or other frozen vegetables substituted. Chow mein noodles or 1/2 cup crushed potato chips can be substituted for shoestring potatoes. 1 1/2 cups cubed, cooked chicken can be substituted for tuna.

Note: Each recipe indicates two cooking times.
The **first** is for a **650**-watt oven.
The **second** (in parentheses) is for an **800**-watt oven.

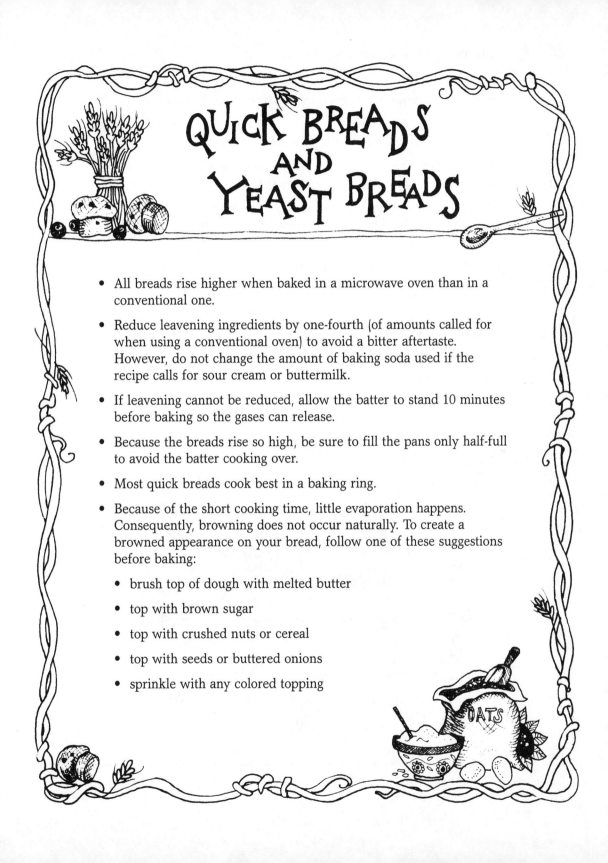

QUICK BREADS AND YEAST BREADS

- All breads rise higher when baked in a microwave oven than in a conventional one.

- Reduce leavening ingredients by one-fourth (of amounts called for when using a conventional oven) to avoid a bitter aftertaste. However, do not change the amount of baking soda used if the recipe calls for sour cream or buttermilk.

- If leavening cannot be reduced, allow the batter to stand 10 minutes before baking so the gases can release.

- Because the breads rise so high, be sure to fill the pans only half-full to avoid the batter cooking over.

- Most quick breads cook best in a baking ring.

- Because of the short cooking time, little evaporation happens. Consequently, browning does not occur naturally. To create a browned appearance on your bread, follow one of these suggestions before baking:

  - brush top of dough with melted butter

  - top with brown sugar

  - top with crushed nuts or cereal

  - top with seeds or buttered onions

  - sprinkle with any colored topping

- top with crumbs made from mixing brown sugar, margarine, and flour

- use a dark flour in the batter instead of white flour

- The most common mistake in making quick breads is overbaking. Follow power levels and baking times carefully.

- Breads are done when the dough recedes from the sides of the pan and springs back when gently touched (even though the surface may appear moist).

- Check for doneness also by inserting a wooden pick in the center of the dough, then checking to see if it comes out clean.

- After baking, cool breads for easier slicing.

- Reheat one piece or slice at a time, wrapped in a paper towel, on High for 15 seconds.

Muffins: Bran, Granola, Grapenuts, Oatmeal, or Wheat Germ

Preparation Time: 20 minutes
Yields 12 muffins

In 2-cup glass measure microwave on high for 1:30 (1:15) minutes:
  1/3 **cup water**

Stir in and let stand 10:00 (8:20) minutes:
  2/3 **cup whole bran cereal, or granola, or grapenuts, or quick-cooking oatmeal, or toasted wheat germ**

Stir together in mixing bowl:
  1 1/4 **cups flour**
  1/3 **cup sugar**
  2 **tsp. baking powder**
  1/4 **tsp. salt**
  1/4 **tsp cinnamon**

Stir together, then stir into dry ingredients just until moistened:
  1 **egg, beaten**
  1/3 **cup milk**
  1/3 **cup cooking oil**
  softened cereal mixture

Fold in:
  1 **small apple, cored and finely chopped, or** 1/3 **cup dried, chopped apricots or raisins**
  1/3 **cup chopped walnuts or pecans**

Fill paper-lined muffin cups half full with batter. Top with crumbs made by combining the following:
  2 **Tbsp. chopped nuts**
  2 **Tbsp. flour**
  1 **Tbsp. brown sugar**
  1 **Tbsp. margarine, melted**

Microwave 6 muffins at a time on High for 3:00 (2:30) minutes or until a wooden pick inserted comes out clean.

Muffin Mix

Prepare mix as directed on package.

Line muffin ring with paper baking cups. Fill half full with batter. Sprinkle tops with cinnamon sugar. Microwave on High for 2:00-3:00 (1:40-2:30) minutes. Serve warm.

Note: Each recipe indicates two cooking times. The **first** is for a **650**-watt oven. The **second** (in parentheses) is for an **800**-watt oven.

Fruit and Spice Muffins

Preparation Time: 8 minutes
Yields 6 muffins

Combine in large mixing bowl:
2/3 cup flour
3 Tbsp. sugar
1 tsp. baking powder
1/4 tsp. salt
1/2 tsp. cinnamon or pumpkin pie spice

Stir into dry ingredients just until moistened:
1 egg yolk, beaten
2 Tbsp. oil
2 Tbsp. milk
1/3 cup applesauce, cooked pumpkin, or mashed bananas

Fold in:
2 Tbsp. chopped nuts or sunflower seeds
2 Tbsp. raisins

Fill paper-lined muffin cups half full. Top with crumbs, chopped nuts, seeds, or cinnamon sugar. Microwave 6 muffins at a time on High for 3:00 (2:30) minutes. Serve warm.

Low-Fat Cornbread

Preparation Time: 17 minutes
6 servings

Combine:
3/4 cup skim milk
1 tsp. vinegar

Mix well. Set aside.

Blend together in large mixing bowl:
1/3 cup cooking oil
1/4 cup sugar

Beat in:
2 egg whites

Stir in milk mixture.

Add:
1 cup unsifted all-purpose flour
2/3 cup yellow cornmeal
1 tsp. baking powder
1/2 tsp. salt
1/4 tsp. baking soda

Mix until smooth.

Use a baking ring or grease bottom and sides of 8-inch round glass baking dish.

Sprinkle with:
cornflake crumbs

If using a baking dish, place a custard cup open-end-up in center of baking dish. Spoon cornbread mixture around cup, spreading evenly.

Microwave uncovered on High for

Note: Each recipe indicates two cooking times.
The **first** is for a **650**-watt oven.
The **second** (in parentheses) is for an **800**-watt oven.

6:00-7:00 (5:00-5:50) minutes or until top is no longer doughy, rotating dish two or three times. Cool 5 minutes. Remove cup and invert cornbread onto serving plate. Cut into wedges.

Note: If cornbread is cooked in baking ring, reduce microwave time to 5:00-6:00 (4:10-5:00) minutes.

Fruity Nut Bread

Preparation Time: 30 minutes
Yields 2 loaves

Beat together in a large mixing bowl:
  2 cups sugar
  1½ cups cooking oil
  3 eggs
  1 tsp. vanilla

Add:
  2 cups strawberries, blueberries, or
  raspberries, thawed
  1 cup nuts, chopped

Stir in:
  3 cups flour
  1 tsp. salt
  1 tsp. baking soda
  1 tsp. cinnamon

Divide batter between two loaf pans which have been greased and coated with finely chopped nuts. Sprinkle chopped nuts on top. Cover with waxed paper and microwave one loaf at a time at 50% for

10:00 (8:20) minutes, then on High for 2:00 (1:40) minutes, or until wooden pick inserted in center comes out clean.

Caramel Nut Sticky Buns

Preparation Time: 10 minutes
6 servings

Combine in 9-inch round baking pan:
  3 Tbsp. margarine
  ⅓ cup brown sugar
  1 Tbsp. water
  1 tsp. cinnamon
  ⅓ cup nuts, chopped

Microwave on High for 60 (50) seconds. Stir to combine, then add:
  1 can refrigerator biscuits, each
  biscuit cut into quarters

Coat each piece in nut mixture. Place in pan, then microwave on High for 2:00-3:00 (1:40-2:30) minutes.

Note: Each recipe indicates two cooking times. The **first** is for a **650**-watt oven. The **second** (in parentheses) is for an **800**-watt oven.

Loaf English Muffins

Preparation Time: 30 minutes
Yields 2 loaves

Grease 2 glass loaf pans and coat with cornmeal.

Combine in mixing bowl:
2 pkgs. dry yeast
3 cups flour
1 Tbsp. sugar
2 tsp. salt
¼ tsp. baking soda

Combine in 4-cup glass measure and heat to 120°F using probe:
2 cups milk
½ cup water

Add liquid ingredients to dry. Beat well and stir in:
2 cups flour

Divide batter between prepared loaf pans and sprinkle with cornmeal. Allow to rise. Cover with waxed paper and microwave each loaf separately on High for 6:00-7:00 (5:00-5:50) minutes. Loaf will look pale. Allow to stand 5 minutes. Slice and toast.

Oatmeal Bread

Preparation Time: 1 hour and 20 minutes
Yields 2 loaves

Combine and allow to stand:
½ cup warm water
2 pkgs. active dry yeast

Combine in large glass mixing bowl and microwave on High for 3:00 (2:30) minutes, uncovered:
1½ cups water
1 cup dry quick cooking oats

Stir in:
⅓ cup margarine, softened
½ cup light molasses
1 Tbsp. salt

Beat in:
2 eggs
2 cups flour

Stir in softened yeast and:
2 cups flour

Stir in an additional:
2 cups flour

Cover with plastic wrap. Microwave at 10% for 10:00 (8:20) minutes. Let stand 20 minutes, or until double in size. Stir down and divide into two buttered loaf pans. Follow same procedure, allowing dough to rise again until double in size. Brush loaves with melted butter and sprinkle with wheat germ or cereal crumbs. Microwave one loaf at a time on High for 8:00-10:00 (6:40-8:20)

Note: Each recipe indicates two cooking times.
The **first** is for a **650**-watt oven.
The **second** (in parentheses) is for an **800**-watt oven.

minutes, or until surface springs back when touched lightly.

Defrosting Frozen Dough

Fill 1-cup glass measure with water. Microwave on High for 3:00 (2:30) minutes. Place frozen dough in greased loaf pan, then place in warm oven beside water. Microwave at 10% for 10:00 (8:20) minutes. Turn dough over. Microwave at 10% for 10:00 (8:20) more minutes. Allow to stand in oven for 30:00 (25:00) minutes, or until dough has risen 1 inch above pan and is ready to bake.

White Bread

Preparation time: 60 minutes
Yields 2 loaves

Heavily butter 2 loaf pans.

Combine in large mixing bowl:
2½ cups all-purpose flour
2 pkgs. dry yeast
2 Tbsp. sugar
2 tsp. salt

Combine in 4-cup glass measure and heat to 125°F, using probe:
1 Tbsp. margarine
2¼ cups milk

Stir liquid mixture into flour mixture and beat well. Knead in until smooth and satiny:
2¾ to 3½ cups flour

Place in greased bowl. To speed bread's rising, place dough in microwave beside 1 cup boiling water. Microwave at 10% for 10:00 (8:20) minutes. Then allow to stand in oven for 20 minutes or until dough has doubled in size.

Form dough into desired shape. Place in greased pan and brush with melted butter to help achieve a more crisp, brown crust. Repeat above procedure so dough rises a second time.

Remove water and microwave bread on High for 6:00-7:00 (5:00-5:50) minutes, or until bread springs back. (This bread may also be baked in a conventional oven, especially if a harder, drier crust is desired.)

Note: Each recipe indicates two cooking times. The **first** is for a **650**-watt oven. The **second** (in parentheses) is for an **800**-watt oven.

Whole Wheat Bread

Preparation Time: 60 minutes
Yields 2 loaves

Follow White Bread recipe (above), except use whole wheat flour in place of all-purpose flour and ¼ cup honey instead of sugar.

Rye Bread

Preparation Time: 60 minutes
Yields 2 loaves

Follow White Bread recipe (see page 111), except use rye flour or pumpernickel flour in place of all-purpose flour and add to dry ingredients:

1 Tbsp. caraway seeds

Defrosting Frozen Breads, Muffins, and Coffee Cakes

An excellent way to keep breads fresh is to freeze them and only defrost what is needed.

Because these baked products defrost very quickly, it is best to defrost them only partially rather than risk their being overcooked.

Wrap breads in paper towels to absorb excess moisture. Use the following guidelines:

Food	Amount	Level	Time
Hamburger buns	1 lb.	30%	3:30 (2:55) minutes
Hot dog buns	1 lb.	30%	3:30 (2:55) minutes
Loaf of bread	1 lb.	80%	1:30 (1:15) minutes
English muffins	2	High	30-45 (25-38) seconds
Pancakes	2	High	30-45 (25-38) seconds
Waffles	2	High	30-45 (25-38) seconds
Coffee cake	12 ozs.	80%	1:30 (1:15) minutes
Tortillas	2	High	15 (13) seconds

Note: Each recipe indicates two cooking times.
The **first** is for a **650**-watt oven.
The **second** (in parentheses) is for an **800**-watt oven.

CAKES, COOKIES AND BARS

What You Ought to Know About Baking Cakes in a Microwave

- Cakes baked in a microwave oven will have a lighter texture and greater volume and be very moist.
- Since microwaved cakes do not brown, dust the greased baking dish with granulated sugar or finely ground nuts before pouring in batter.
- Since cakes rise higher when microwaved, pour in only enough batter to make the baking dish one-third to one-half full.
- For a special treat, divide the extra cake batter into cupcake pans or flat-bottomed ice cream cups and microwave on High for 50 (42) seconds.
- Always cover a cake with waxed paper or a paper towel to allow steam to escape, but to keep the heat in.
- Always start on the lower power level indicated so the cake doesn't get tough.
- Be careful not to overbake. Follow the shortest baking time suggested. Check with a tester, then bake the additional suggested time if needed.
- Frost or cover the cake as soon as possible after cooling, since a crustless cake tends to get stale quickly.

- Some items work better in conventional ovens. For example, chiffon and angel food cakes do not microwave well.
- Many cakes mixes now include microwave directions.

Preparing a Basic Cake Mix

Because speed is important to most microwave-oven users, here are instructions for doing a basic cake mix, with a series of delicious variations.

"From scratch" cakes can also be done in a microwave oven, although without the efficiency possible with a mix. So take your pick!

- Mix the ingredients together about 5 minutes before you plan to bake the cake so the leavening has a chance to react to the moisture before it is heated.
- Use 1 less egg than called for by instructions for a conventional oven. The reason? The steam that is created in the microwave process produces extra leavening power (see page 116).
- Use one-fourth less water than called for by instructions for a conventional oven. In a conventional oven some of the moisture evaporates during the dry heat process, but in the shortened microwave process there is not time for this to happen (see page 116).

Note: Each recipe indicates two cooking times.
The **first** is for a **650**-watt oven.
The **second** (in parentheses) is for an **800**-watt oven.

- Fill the prepared pan only half full. With the extra volume produced by the microwave process, this is essential or the batter will run over.
- Cover with waxed paper or a paper towel to keep the heat in the product while allowing the steam to escape.
- Depending on the mix the cake will bake in 10:00-15:00 (8:20-12:30) minutes at 70%. After 10 minutes, test for doneness, then add more cooking time if necessary.
- To test for doneness, insert the tester into the center of the cake. If it comes out clean, the cake is done. The cake may appear moist and still be finished. The extra moisture will disappear during the standing time. If the cake begins to pull away from the sides of the pan, it is done.
- Usually a cake requires the same amount of standing time as baking time. If possible, let a cake stand in the oven because the extra heat on the bottom will help the extra moisture to evaporate.
- Frosting or glazing a cake is highly recommended, since a cake does not develop a crust when baked in a microwave and so has a tendency to become stale rather quickly.

Making Cupcakes

- Fill paper-lined muffin cups half full with cake batter.
- Microwave 6 cupcakes at a time, on High for 2:00-3:00 (1:40-2:30) minutes, or until an inserted wooden pick comes out clean. (Flat-bottomed ice cream cups can be substituted for the cake papers.)

A Word about Baking Pans

Round pans bake better than square pans, because food in corners tends to dry out since it is hit first by the microwaves.

A tube pan is ideal. It distributes the heat more evenly due to the fact that microwaves cook from the outside in, as well as the inside out.

If you don't have a baking ring, a glass tumbler inverted in a large round casserole dish will serve the same purpose. On the other hand, baking rings are very inexpensive and can be used for more than just baking cakes.

Note: Each recipe indicates two cooking times. The **first** is for a **650**-watt oven. The **second** (in parentheses) is for an **800**-watt oven.

Preparing the Pan

Grease the pan as you would for use in a conventional oven. Sprinkle with an ingredient that will give the color and texture you desire for your finished produce.
- Granulated sugar will produce a sweet crisp crust.
- Brownulated sugar will produce a sweet, brown, crisp crust.
- Cinnamon sugar will produce a spicy, sweet-flavored crust.
- Finely ground nuts, cereal, or graham cracker crumbs will produce a crisper, browner crust.

Defrosting a Frozen Cake

- Cakes defrost very quickly. But watch the time and power level to avoid producing a tough and rubbery texture.
- Defrost at 30% power.
- Cover with either waxed paper or a paper towel to retain moisture.
- A pound cake takes 2:00 (1:40) minutes for a 10¾-oz. cake

- 1 2- or 3-layer cake weighing 1 lb. takes 2:00-3:00 (1:40-2:30) minutes.
- Cupcakes take 15-30 (13-25) seconds apiece, if done one at a time.

Basic Cake Mix, adapted for a microwave oven

(Use these instructions for a cake mix in which the conventional directions call for 3 eggs, 1 cup water, ⅓ cup oil)

Preparation Time: 15 minutes
Yields 1 cake

Combine in mixing bowl:
  2 eggs
  ¾ cup water
  ⅓ cup oil
  1 cake mix

Pour into greased and sugar-sprinkled microwave-safe tube pan.

Microwave on High for 5:00 (4:10) minutes. Microwave at 70% for 7:00 (5:50) minutes more. Test for doneness.

Note: Each recipe indicates two cooking times.
The **first** is for a **650**-watt oven.
The **second** (in parentheses) is for an **800**-watt oven.

Instant Glazed Cake

Preparation Time: 18 minutes
Yields 1 cake

Grease and sugar 12-cup microwave-safe baking ring.

In 2-cup glass measure microwave on High for 45 (38) seconds:
 ¼ cup margarine

Add and mix well:
 **¾ cup preserves (orange or
  raspberry)**
 ½ cup coconut, flaked

Spread evenly over the bottom of the prepared pan.

Spoon favorite prepared cake mix over top.

Cover and bake as directed for cake mix (see page 116).

Ganache

Combine in 4-cup glass measuring cup:
 2 cups chocolate chips
 1 cup whipping cream

Microwave and stir until smooth.

Pour over cake or allow to set up and pipe on as decorations.

Easy Chocolate Frosting

Preparation Time: 6 minutes
Yields 1¾ cups

Combine in 4-cup glass measuring cup and microwave on High for 3:00-4:00 (2:30-3:20) minutes, stirring twice during that time:
 1 cup sugar
 ¼ cup margarine
 ¼ cup milk

Then stir in:
 ⅔ cup chocolate pieces

Stir 2 or 3 times until thickened, then spread on cake.

Note: Each recipe indicates two cooking times.
The **first** is for a **650**-watt oven.
The **second** (in parentheses) is for an **800**-watt oven.

Vanilla Frosting

Preparation Time: 5 minutes
Yields frosting for one layer cake

Soften (without melting) in microwave at
30% for 60 (50) seconds:
   3 Tbsp. butter

Beat in:
   1 cup confectioners' sugar, sifted
   1 Tbsp. light cream

When smooth, stir in:
   3/4 tsp. vanilla

Spread over cake before frosting hardens.

German Chocolate
Cake Topping

Microwave for 3:00 (2:30) minutes in 8-cup
glass measure:
   1 cup evaporated milk
   1 cup brown sugar
   3 egg yolks, well beaten
   1/2 cup margarine

Stir and microwave at 60 (50)-second
intervals until sauce begins to thicken.

Stir in:
   1 tsp. vanilla
   1 1/3 cups shredded coconut
   1 cup chopped pecans

Peanut Butter Frosting

Preparation Time: 5 minutes
Yields frosting for one layer cake

In 4-cup glass microwave-safe measuring
bowl microwave at 50% for 1:00-2:00
(50 seconds-1:40) minutes, or until mixture
comes to boil:
   2 Tbsp. butter or margarine
   2 Tbsp. peanut butter
   2 Tbsp. milk or cream
   1/8 tsp. salt

Stir in:
   2 cups confectioners' sugar
   1/2 tsp. vanilla

Beat until smooth. Spread over cake before
frosting hardens.

Note: Each recipe indicates two cooking times.
The **first** is for a **650**-watt oven.
The **second** (in parentheses) is for an **800**-watt oven.

Dark Chocolate Cake

Preparation Time: 30 minutes
Yields 1 cake

In 8-cup glass measure microwave on High
for 45 (38) seconds:
  ⅓ cup margarine

Beat in:
  1 cup sugar
  1 tsp. vanilla

Add and mix well:
  1 egg
  1½ cups milk
  1½ cups flour
  ½ cup unsweetened cocoa
  ½ tsp. baking soda
  ½ tsp. baking powder
  ½ tsp. salt

Pour evenly into greased and sugared pan
and cover with waxed paper. Microwave at
50% for 14:00 (11:40) minutes. Test for
doneness and microwave in 60 (50)-second
increments until tester comes out clean
(surface will look moist). Let stand 10
minutes. Frost or cover as soon as cool.

Pound Cake

Preparation Time: 20 minutes
Yields 1 cake

Grease glass loaf pan, then sprinkle with
finely ground almonds.

Microwave in glass mixing bowl for 30 (25)
seconds:
  ½ cup butter

Cream in:
  1 cup sugar
  2 eggs

Add and mix until smooth:
  ½ cup milk
  ½ tsp. vanilla
  1¼ cups flour
  ½ tsp. baking powder
  ¼ tsp. salt

Spoon batter evenly into prepared loaf pan.
Cover with waxed paper. Microwave at 50%
for 10:00 (8:20) minutes. Test for doneness
and microwave on High for
30 (25)-second increments until tester
inserted in center comes out clean.

Note: Each recipe indicates two cooking times.
The **first** is for a **650**-watt oven.
The **second** (in parentheses) is for an **800**-watt oven.

Crowned Pound Cake

Preparation Time: 35 minutes
Yields 1 cake

To make topping, microwave on High for 15-20 (13-17) seconds:
1/3 cup butter

Stir in:
2 Tbsp. brown sugar
1/2 cup pecans, chopped
3/4 cup vanilla wafers, crushed

Grease bottom and sides of glass loaf dish, then line the bottom with waxed paper. Pat topping evenly into bottom and up the sides. In glass measuring bowl, microwave on High for 20-30 (17-25) seconds:
1/2 cup butter

Cream in:
1 cup sugar
2 eggs

Add and mix until smooth:
1/2 cup milk
1/2 tsp. vanilla
1 1/4 cups flour
1/2 tsp. baking powder
1/2 tsp. salt

Pour batter evenly into prepared pan. Microwave at 50% power for 10:00 (8:20) minutes, then on High for 2:00-3:00 (1:40-2:30) minutes, or until a toothpick inserted in center comes out clean. Cool 15 minutes. Serve with ice cream.

Poppy Seed Ring Cake

Preparation Time: 25 minutes
10-12 servings

Combine in large mixer bowl:
18 1/2-oz. pkg. yellow cake mix
3 3/4-oz. pkg. lemon instant pudding and pie filling mix
4 eggs
1/2 cup cooking oil
1 cup (less 1 1/2 Tbsp.) water
1/3 cup poppy seeds

Beat mixture at low speed with an electric mixer until ingredients are moistened, then beat on high speed 3-4 minutes. If beating by hand, stir until ingredients are moistened; then beat about 150 strokes per minute for 3-4 minutes. Butter the bottom and sides of a 10-cup glass or plastic ring mold with:
1 Tbsp. butter or margarine

Mix and sprinkle on bottom and sides:
1 Tbsp. cinnamon
3 Tbsp. granulated sugar

Remove 1 cup of batter from mixer bowl and save to make cupcakes. Pour remaining batter into mold.

Microwave at 50% for 10:00 (8:20) minutes, then on High for 2:00 (1:40) minutes. Let cake stand in oven 5 minutes, until it begins to pull away from sides. Remove from oven and invert cake onto serving plate.

Note: Each recipe indicates two cooking times.
The **first** is for a **650**-watt oven.
The **second** (in parentheses) is for an **800**-watt oven.

Creme de Menthe Cake

Preparation Time: 30 minutes
Yields 1 cake

Grease and sugar 12-cup baking ring.

Combine in large mixer bowl:
  18½-oz. pkg. yellow cake mix
  3½-oz. pkg. pistachio pudding mix
  1 cup cooking oil
  ¾ cup water
  ¼ cup creme de menthe
  4 eggs

Blend with an electric mixer until moistened, then beat on high for 3 minutes. Pour evenly into prepared pan.

Pour over batter and stir to marble:
  ½ cup chocolate syrup

Cover with waxed paper. Microwave at 50% for 12:00 (10:00) minutes, then on High for 3:00-4:00 (2:30-3:20) minutes, or until a wooden pick comes out clean. Let stand in microwave for 10:00 (8:20) minutes. Cool. Frost.

Piña Colada Cake

Preparation Time: 30 minutes
Yields 1 cake

Combine in large mixer bowl:
  18½-oz. pkg. yellow cake mix
  3½-oz. pkg. coconut pudding mix
  1 cup cooking oil
  ¾ cup water
  ¼ cup dark rum, or
    1 Tbsp. rum flavoring
  4 eggs

Blend with electric mixer until moistened, then beat on high for 3 minutes. Pour evenly into greased and lightly sugared 9 x 13 pan. Cover with waxed paper. Microwave at 50% for 12:00 (10:00) minutes, then on High for 3:00-4:00 (2:30-3:20) minutes, or until a wooden pick comes out clean. Let stand 10 minutes. Frost with frosting made by combining:
  3½-oz. pkg. coconut pudding mix
  1 container whipped topping, thawed
  1 can crushed pineapple
  ¼ cup dark rum, or
    1 Tbsp. rum flavoring

Note: Each recipe indicates two cooking times. The **first** is for a **650**-watt oven. The **second** (in parentheses) is for an **800**-watt oven.

Thumbprint Cookies

Preparation Time: 10 minutes
Yields 36-40 cookies

Beat together to form firm dough:
   1/2 cup butter, softened
   1/4 cup brown sugar
   1 egg
   1 tsp. vanilla
   1 1/2 cups flour
   1/4 tsp. salt
   1 1/2 cups coconut

Form into 3/4-inch balls, then place 16 cookies in a circle on microwave-safe baking sheet or piece of cardboard. Flatten each cookie with thumb. Microwave on High for 2:00-4:00 (1:40-3:20) minutes. Fill imprints with jelly or icing.

Hello Dolly's

Preparation Time: 25 minutes
Yields 24 bars

In 9-inch round dish microwave on High for 1:30 (1:15) minutes:
   6 Tbsp. butter

Spread over melted butter:
   1 cup graham cracker crumbs

Sprinkle over crumbs:
   3 1/2 ozs. coconut, grated

Layer:
   6 ozs. chocolate chips
   6 ozs. peanut butter chips
   1 cup nuts, chopped

Pour over all:
   1 can sweetened condensed milk
   (see page 151)

Microwave at 70% for 9:00-10:00 (7:30-8:20) minutes. Let stand 10 minutes.

Peanut Butter Bars

Preparation Time: 20 minutes
Yields 24 bars

Blend until smooth:
   1 cup margarine, softened
   1 cup brown sugar
   1/4 cup peanut butter

Mix in until combined:
   1 3/4 cups flour
   1 cup dry rolled oats
   1/2 tsp. baking soda

Press mixture into greased 8 x 12 glass baking pan. Microwave at 70% for 7:00-9:00 (5:50-7:30) minutes, or until puffed in center. Set aside. Combine in glass measure and microwave on High for 2:00-3:00 (1:40-2:30) minutes, or until melted:
   1/3 cup semi-sweet chocolate pieces
   3 Tbsp. peanut butter

Spread over baked bars. Cool and cut.

Note: Each recipe indicates two cooking times.
The **first** is for a **650**-watt oven.
The **second** (in parentheses) is for an **800**-watt oven.

Coconut Macaroons

Preparation Time: 12 minutes
Yields 3 dozen cookies

Combine in 2-quart glass mixing bowl:
2²/₃ cups flaked coconut
²/₃ cup sweetened condensed milk
(see recipe on page 151, or use half
a can prepared milk)
1 tsp. vanilla or almond extract

Microwave on High for 2:00 (1:40) minutes.
Stir. Microwave on High another 2:00 (1:40)
minutes. Stir. Microwave on High 2:00
(1:40) minutes more, or until mixture loses
its gloss. Immediately spoon onto waxed
paper and shape into balls. Store in airtight
container.

Favorite Chocolate Brownies

Preparation Time: 20 minutes
12-16 servings

Place in 1-quart glass mixing bowl:
¼ cup butter or margarine

Microwave uncovered on High for 15-20
(12-15) seconds, or until softened.

Blend in:
½ cup sugar

Add, one at a time, beating after each:
2 eggs

Blend in:
½ tsp. vanilla

Add:
½ cup unsifted all-purpose flour
½ cup chocolate-flavored ice cream
syrup
¼ tsp. salt

Mix well. If desired, add ⅓ cup chopped
nuts.

Grease bottom only of 8-inch square
microwave-safe baking dish. Spread batter
in dish and cover loosely with plastic wrap.

Microwave on High for 5:00-6:00
(4:10-5:00) minutes, or until no longer
doughy, rotating dish once or twice. Let
stand in microwave oven for 10 minutes.
Uncover and cool. Cut into squares.

Note: Each recipe indicates two cooking times.
The **first** is for a **650**-watt oven.
The **second** (in parentheses) is for an **800**-watt oven.

Chewy Gooey Bars

Preparation Time: 15 minutes
Yields 24 bars

Combine in 2-quart glass measure:
2 cups quick dry oats
1/2 cup margarine

Microwave on High for 3:00-4:00
(2:30-3:20) minutes and then stir in:
1/2 cup brown sugar, packed
1/4 cup light corn syrup
1/4 cup peanut butter, optional

Microwave on High for 2:00-3:00
(1:40-2:30) minutes, or until sugar is melted,
then press mixture into buttered baking
dish

Place in 1-cup glass measure and
microwave on High for 2:00 (1:40) minutes,
or until smooth when stirred:
1/3 cup semi-sweet chocolate pieces
2 Tbsp. peanut butter

Spread over warm mixture. Chill and cut
into squares.

*Note: To fill a 9 x 13 baking dish, double the
recipe.*

Cherry Chocolate Brownies

Preparation Time: 20 minutes
12-16 servings

Place in 1-quart glass mixing bowl:
1/3 cup butter or margarine

Microwave uncovered on High for 45-60
(38-50) seconds, or until melted.

Stir in:
1/3 cup unsweetened cocoa powder
1 cup sugar

Add, one at a time, beating after each:
2 eggs

Blend in:
1/2 tsp. vanilla

Add:
3/4 cup unsifted all-purpose flour
1/2 tsp. baking powder

Mix well. Grease bottom only of 8-inch
square microwave-safe baking dish. Spread
batter in dish.

Sprinkle with:
1/3 cup chopped maraschino cherries

Cover loosely with plastic wrap. Microwave
on High for 5:00-6:00 (4:10-5:00) minutes,
or until no longer doughy, rotating dish
once or twice. Let stand in microwave oven
for 10 minutes. Uncover, cool, and cut into
squares.

Note: Each recipe indicates two cooking times.
The **first** is for a **650**-watt oven.
The **second** (in parentheses) is for an **800**-watt oven.

Peanut Butter Brownies

Preparation Time: 25 minutes
12-16 servings

Combine in 1-quart glass mixing bowl:
**2 squares (2 ozs.) unsweetened
    chocolate**
1/4 cup butter or margarine

Microwave uncovered on High for
1:00-1:30 (50 seconds-1:15) minutes, or until
melted, stirring once.

Blend in:
1 cup sugar

Add, one at a time, beating after each:
2 eggs

Blend in:
1/2 tsp. vanilla

Add:
3/4 cup unsifted all-purpose flour
1/2 tsp. baking powder
1/4 tsp. salt

Mix well. Grease bottom only of 8-inch
square microwave-safe baking dish. Spread
batter in dish. Set aside.

Place in 1-cup glass measure:
**1/3 cup chunky or creamy peanut
    butter**

Microwave uncovered on High for
1:00-1:30 minutes (50 seconds-1:15
minutes), or until hot, stirring once. Spoon
over batter. Cover loosely with plastic wrap.

Microwave on High for 5:00-6:00
(4:10-5:00) minutes, or until no longer
doughy, rotating dish once or twice. Let
stand in microwave oven for 10 minutes.
Uncover, cool, and cut into squares. If
desired, frost and top with crushed peanuts.

Note: Each recipe indicates two cooking times.
The **first** is for a **650**-watt oven.
The **second** (in parentheses) is for an **800**-watt oven.

Macadamia Nut Brownies

Preparation Time: 20 minutes
12-16 servings

Combine in 1-quart glass mixing bowl:
6 Tbsp. butter or margarine
1/2 cup semi-sweet chocolate pieces

Microwave uncovered on High for
1:00-1:30 (50 seconds-1:15) minutes, or until
melted, stirring once.

Blend in:
1 cup sugar

Add, one at a time, beating after each:
~~**2 eggs**~~

Blend in:
1 tsp. vanilla

Add:
1 1/2 cups unsifted all-purpose flour
1/2 tsp. baking powder
1/4 tsp. salt

Mix well.

Stir in:
1/3 cup macadamia nuts, coarsely chopped

Grease bottom only of 8-inch square
microwave-safe baking dish. Spread batter
in dish. Cover loosely with plastic wrap.

Microwave on High for 5:00-6:00
(4:10-5:00) minutes, or until no longer

doughy, rotating dish once or twice. Let
stand in microwave oven for 10 minutes.
Uncover and cool.

Sprinkle with:
powdered sugar

Cut into squares.

*Note: Other nuts can be substituted for
macadamia nuts.*

Chewy Butterscotch Brownies

Preparation Time: 20 minutes
12-16 servings

Place in 1-quart glass mixing bowl:
1/3 cup butter or margarine

Microwave uncovered on High for 20-30
(17-25) seconds, or until softened.

Blend in:
1 cup packed brown sugar

Add, one at a time, beating after each:
2 eggs

Blend in:
1 tsp. vanilla

Add:
1 cup unsifted all-purpose flour
1/2 tsp. baking powder
1/4 tsp. salt

Mix well.

Note: Each recipe indicates two cooking times.
The **first** is for a **650**-watt oven.
The **second** (in parentheses) is for an **800**-watt oven.

Stir in:
½ cup nuts, chopped
¼ cup butterscotch pieces

Grease bottom only of 8-inch square microwave-safe baking dish. Spread batter in dish.

Sprinkle with:
¼ cup butterscotch pieces
(additional)

Cover loosely with plastic wrap.

Microwave on High for 5:00-6:00 (4:10-5:00) minutes, or until no longer doughy, rotating dish once or twice. Let stand in microwave oven for 10 minutes. Uncover and cool. Cut into squares.

Cream Cheese Brownies

Preparation Time: 25 minutes
12-16 servings

Place in 1-quart glass mixing bowl:
½ cup butter or margarine

Microwave uncovered on High for 20-30 (17-25) seconds, or until softened.

Blend in:
1 cup sugar

Add, one at a time, beating after each:
2 eggs

Blend in:
1 tsp. vanilla

Add:
¾ cup unsifted all-purpose flour
⅓ cup unsweetened cocoa powder
½ tsp. baking powder
¼ tsp. salt

Mix well. Grease bottom only of 8-inch square microwave-safe baking dish. Spread half of batter in dish. Set aside.

Place in 2-cup glass measure:
3-oz. pkg. cream cheese

Microwave on High for 30-45 (25-38) seconds, or until softened.

Blend in:
1 Tbsp. sugar

Spoon over batter in dish. Spoon remaining batter evenly over top. Cut through batter with knife several times to marble. Cover loosely with plastic wrap. Microwave on High for 5:30-6:30 (4:35-5:25) minutes, or until no longer doughy, rotating dish once or twice. Let stand in microwave oven for 10 minutes. Uncover and cool. Cut into squares.

Note: Each recipe indicates two cooking times. The **first** is for a **650**-watt oven. The **second** (in parentheses) is for an **800**-watt oven.

Macaroon Brownies

Preparation Time: 20 minutes
12-15 servings

Combine in 1-quart glass bowl:
**2 squares (2 ozs.) unsweetened
    chocolate**
¼ cup butter or margarine

Microwave uncovered on High for
1:00-1:30 (50 seconds-1:15) minutes, or until
melted, stirring once. Blend in:
1 cup sugar

Add, one at a time, beating after each:
2 eggs

Blend in:
1 tsp. vanilla

Add:
¾ cup unsifted all-purpose flour
½ tsp. baking powder

Mix well. Grease 10 x 6-inch microwave-
safe baking dish on bottom only. Spread
batter in dish. Set aside.

Combine:
1 cup coconut, flaked
¼ cup light corn syrup
1 Tbsp. flour
1 Tbsp. half-and-half or milk
¼ tsp. almond extract

Mix well. Drop by teaspoonfuls onto bars.
Swirl knife through batter several times.
Cover loosely with plastic wrap.

Microwave on High for 5:30-6:30
(4:35-5:25) minutes, or until no longer
doughy, rotating dish once or twice. Let
stand in microwave oven for 10 minutes.

Uncover and cool. If desired, frost with
favorite chocolate frosting. Cut into squares
and serve.

*Note: If desired, add ⅓ cup chopped nuts to
batter just before spreading in pan.*

Note: Each recipe indicates two cooking times.
The **first** is for a **650**-watt oven.
The **second** (in parentheses) is for an **800**-watt oven.

Rocky Ridge Brownies

Preparation Time: 25 minutes
12-16 servings

Combine in 1-quart glass mixing bowl:
1 1/2 squares (1 1/2 ozs.) unsweetened chocolate
1/3 cup butter or margarine

Microwave uncovered on High for 1:00-1:30 (50 seconds-1:15) minutes, or until melted, stirring once.

Blend in:
1 cup sugar

Add, one at a time, beating after each:
2 eggs

Blend in:
1 tsp. vanilla

Add:
1 cup unsifted all-purpose flour
1/2 tsp. baking powder
1/4 tsp. salt

Mix well.

Stir in:
1/4 cup pecans or walnuts, chopped

Grease bottom only of 8-inch square microwave-safe baking dish. Spread batter in dish. Cover loosely with plastic wrap.

Microwave on High for 5:00-6:00 (4:10-5:00) minutes, or until no longer doughy, rotating dish once or twice.

Sprinkle evenly with:
2 cups miniature marshmallows

Cover and let stand in microwave oven for 10 minutes. Uncover and cool.

Meanwhile, combine in 2-cup glass measure:
1/2 square (1/2 oz.) unsweetened chocolate
1 Tbsp. butter or margarine

Microwave uncovered on High for 45-60 (38-50) seconds, or until melted, stirring once.

Beat in:
1/2 cup unsifted confectioners' sugar
1/4 tsp. vanilla

Add, until of a glaze consistency:
1-2 tsp. hot water

Drizzle evenly over brownies. Cool completely. Cut into squares using knife dipped in hot water.

Note: Each recipe indicates two cooking times.
The **first** is for a **650**-watt oven.
The **second** (in parentheses) is for an **800**-watt oven.

Caramel Brownies

Preparation Time: 23 minutes
12-16 servings

Combine in 1-quart glass mixing bowl:
**2 squares (2 ozs.) unsweetened
  chocolate**
½ cup butter or margarine

Microwave uncovered on High for 1:00-1:30
(50 seconds-1:15) minutes, or until melted,
stirring once.

Blend in:
½ cup sugar
½ cup packed brown sugar

Add, one at a time, beating after each:
2 eggs

Blend in:
1 tsp. vanilla

Add:
1 cup unsifted all-purpose flour
½ tsp. baking powder

Mix well. Grease bottom only of 8-inch
square microwave-safe baking dish. Spread
half of batter in dish.

Drizzle with:
½ cup caramel ice cream topping

Sprinkle with:
⅓ cup chopped nuts

Spoon remaining batter evenly over caramel
and nuts. Cover loosely with plastic wrap.

Microwave on High for 4:00 (3:20) minutes,
or until no longer doughy, rotating dish
once or twice. Let stand in microwave oven
for 10 minutes. Uncover and cool. Cut into
squares.

Note: Each recipe indicates two cooking times.
The **first** is for a **650**-watt oven.
The **second** (in parentheses) is for an **800**-watt oven.

PIES AND DESSERTS

Apple or Peach Crumb Pie

Preparation Time: 20 minutes
6-8 servings

Cover bottom of unbaked 9-inch pie crust with dried beans or rice, or set an empty glass casserole dish within it. Then microwave crust on High for 3-5 (2:55-4:10) minutes.

Peel and slice:
2 lbs. apples or peaches

Sprinkle fruit with:
2 tsp. lemon juice

Combine and toss with fruit:
½ cup brown sugar
½ Tbsp. cornstarch
½ tsp. cinnamon

Arrange in pie crust. Cover with waxed paper and microwave on High for 4:00-6:00 (3:20-5:00) minutes, or until fruit is tender.

Sprinkle with crumb topping made by combining:
½ cup flour
⅓ cup brown sugar
¼ cup margarine, softened
¼ tsp. cinnamon
⅓ cup nuts, finely chopped (optional)

Microwave on High for 4:00-6:00 (3:20-5:00) minutes, or until set.

Strawberry or Blueberry Pie

Preparation Time: 10 minutes
(Chillling Time: 2 hours)
Yields 1 pie

Combine in 4-cup glass measuring cup:
1 cup strawberries or blueberries
1 cup water
1 cup sugar

Microwave on High until boiling, about 5:00 (4:10) minutes. Strain berries from juice and slowly stir into juice:
3 Tbsp. cornstarch, dissolved in
⅓ cup cold water

Microwave until thick and clear, stirring at 1-minute intervals. Chill, then pour over:
1 quart berries

Pour into 9-inch baked pie shell.

Top with whipped cream and serve immediately.

Note: Each recipe indicates two cooking times.
The **first** is for a **650**-watt oven.
The **second** (in parentheses) is for an **800**-watt oven.

Pecan Pie

Preparation Time: 35 minutes
Yields 1 pie

In medium glass mixing bowl, microwave at 70% for 60 (50) seconds, or until melted:
2 Tbsp. butter or margarine

Stir in and mix well:
3 eggs, slightly beaten
1 cup dark corn syrup
1/4 cup brown sugar
1 1/2 tsp. all-purpose flour
1 tsp. vanilla
1 1/2 cups pecan halves

Pour filling into 9-inch unbaked shell. Microwave at 30% for 25:00-30:00 (20:50-25:00) minutes, or until knife inserted near the center comes out clean. Cool.

Lemon Meringue Pie

Preparation Time: 15 minutes
6-8 servings

Combine:
2 1/4 cups sugar
1/2 cup cornstarch

Stir in:
2 1/4 cups water

Microwave on High for 3:00 (2:30) minutes. Stir.

Beat and gradually combine with hot mixture:
4 egg yolks

Microwave on High for 2:00 (1:40) minutes. Stir. Microwave on High 2:00 (1:40) more minutes. Stir. Continue process until mixture thickens.

Stir in:
1/4 cup butter
3 Tbsp. lemon juice
1 Tbsp. lemon rind

Pour into:
9-inch baked pie crust

Top with meringue made by beating to soft peaks:
3 egg whites
1/4 tsp. cream of tartar

Add and beat until stiff peaks form:
3/4 tsp. vanilla
6 Tbsp. sugar, added 1 Tbsp.
at a time

Microwave on High for 2:00 (1:40) minutes, until egg whites are set. The meringue will not brown unless it is sprayed with a solution made by dissolving brown sugar in water.

Note: Microwave lemon for 20 (17) seconds before squeezing to release more juice. Also, scrape the outside of the lemon before squeezing with a sharp paring knife to release the oils which contain the flavor of the rind. Use these oils rather than the rind for a smoother filling.

Note: Each recipe indicates two cooking times. The **first** is for a **650**-watt oven. The **second** (in parentheses) is for an **800**-watt oven.

Lemon Chiffon Pie

Preparation Time: 7 minutes
6-8 servings

Beat until stiff and set aside:
4 egg whites
½ cup sugar

Combine until softened:
1 Tbsp. unflavored gelatin
½ cup cold water

In 2-quart glass measure combine:
4 eggs yolks
½ cup sugar
½ cup lemon juice
½ tsp. salt

Microwave on High for 2:00 (1:40) minutes. Stir in softened gelatin mixture and:
1 Tbsp. lemon rind

Fold in egg-white mixture and serve in:
9-inch baked pie shell

Coconut Cream Pie

Preparation Time: 30 minutes
Yields 1 pie

Combine in a 9-inch glass pie pan:
1 square semi-sweet chocolate
¼ cup butter

Microwave on High for 1:00-1:30 (50 seconds-1:15) minutes. Stir in:
2 cups coconut, flaked

Microwave on High for 2:00-2:30 (1:40-2:05) minutes. Cool. Remove ½ cup and reserve for topping.

Press remainder of coconut mixture onto bottom and sides of pan to form a crust.

Combine in 1-quart glass measure;
½ cup sugar
¼ cup cornstarch
2 cups milk
½ tsp. salt

Microwave on High for 7:00-8:00 (5:50-6:40) minutes, or until mixture thickens and boils. Stir twice during cooking time.

Beat:
2 eggs

Gradually stir warm mixture into eggs.

Microwave on High for 60 (50) seconds, until mixture bubbles. Stir in:
2 Tbsp. butter
2 Tbsp. rum or ½ tsp. rum flavoring

Note: Each recipe indicates two cooking times.
The **first** is for a **650**-watt oven.
The **second** (in parentheses) is for an **800**-watt oven.

Cool 15 minutes. Spoon into coconut crust and top with whipped topping and reserved coconut mixture.

Coconut Custard Pie

Preparation Time: 20 minutes
8-10 minutes

Beat until smooth in mixer or blender:
1/4 cup butter
4 eggs
2 cups milk
1/4 cup honey
1/2 cup flour
1/2 tsp. baking powder
1/2 tsp. salt
1 1/2 tsp. vanilla
1 1/2 tsp. orange peel, grated
1/4 cup orange juice

Stir in:
1 cup flaked coconut

Pour into greased 9- or 10-inch glass pie plate. Top with cinnamon sugar. Microwave on High for 8:00-10:00 (6:40-8:20) minutes, or until edges are set, then at 50% for 5:00-6:00 (4:10-5:00) minutes, or until center is puffed and set.

Pumpkin Pie Bake

Preparation Time: 20 minutes
6-8 servings

Combine in blender and blend for 60 (50) seconds:
3/4 cup evaporated milk
3/4 cup sugar
1/2 cup buttermilk baking mix
2 Tbsp. butter
2 eggs
2 cups processed pumpkin
2 1/2 tsp. pumpkin pie spice
2 tsp. vanilla

Pour into greased 9-inch glass pie plate. Cover with tented waxed paper. Microwave on High for 8:00-10:00 (6:40-8:20) minutes or until edges are set, then at 50% for 5:00-6:00 (4:10-5:00) minutes, or until center is set.

Note: Each recipe indicates two cooking times. The **first** is for a **650**-watt oven. The **second** (in parentheses) is for an **800**-watt oven.

Grasshopper Pie

Preparation Time: 40 minutes
6-8 servings

To form crust, microwave in a 9-inch glass pie plate on High for 30 (25) seconds:
   3 Tbsp. butter or margarine

Stir in:
   1½ cups chocolate cream-filled cookies (15-20), crumbled

Press into bottom and up the sides of dish. Microwave on High for 2:00 (1:40) minutes. Cool. Set aside.

In a large mixing bowl combine:
   30 large or 3 cups miniature marshmallows
   ½ cup milk

Microwave on High for 2:00 (1:40) minutes, or until marshmallows begin to puff. Stir. If marshmallows are not completely melted, cook a few more seconds.

Stir in:
   2-3 Tbsp. creme de cocoa
   2-3 Tbsp. creme de menthe

Cool about 30 minutes, until mixture is thickened but not set. Fold in:
   1 cup whipping cream, whipped

Pour mixture into cooled crust. Refrigerate 4-6 hours, or until well chilled.

Garnish with whipped cream and chocolate curls if desired.

Note: You may use white creme de menthe, but, if you do, add 4-5 drops green food coloring. This pie will not keep for more than 2 days.

Fruit Crisp

Preparation Time: 15 minutes
6-8 servings

Microwave on High for 30 (25) seconds in 2-quart glass measure:
   ¼ cup margarine

Stir in until crumbly:
   ¾ cup brown sugar
   ¾ cup flour
   2 Tbsp. flaked coconut
   2 Tbsp. chopped nuts
   1 tsp. cinnamon

Combine half of crumb mixture with:
   4 cups apples, cherries, or peaches

Place in round baking dish. Top with remaining crumbs. Cover with waxed paper. Microwave on High for 10-12 (8:20-10:00) minutes, or until set.

Note: Each recipe indicates two cooking times. The **first** is for a **650**-watt oven. The **second** (in parentheses) is for an **800**-watt oven.

Apple Crisp

Preparation Time: 20 minutes
6-8 servings

Combine in 8-inch square pan:
5 cups sliced apples
½ cup raisins

Cover with plastic wrap and microwave on High for 5:00-6:00 (4:10-5:00) minutes. Set aside.

In small mixing bowl combine:
1 cup flour
½ cup sugar
½ tsp. baking powder
¼ tsp. salt
1 egg

Mix until crumbly and sprinkle over apples. Set aside.

Microwave in 1-cup glass measure for 30 (25) seconds:
⅓ cup butter

Drizzle over crumbs then sprinkle with:
cinnamon

Microwave on High for 5:00-6:00 (4:10-5:00) minutes, or until topping is no longer doughy.

Pretzel Salad

Mix together and press into 9 x 13 pan:
2 cups crushed pretzels
¾ cup melted butter
3 Tbsp. sugar

Microwave on High for 1:30 (1:15) minutes. Set aside.

In mixer bowl, beat together:
8 oz. cream cheese, softened
8 oz. whipped topping, thawed
1 cup sugar

Pour over pretzel crust.

Dissolve:
2 small boxes strawberry gelatin in
2 cups boiling water

Stir in:
20 ozs. frozen strawberries.

Refrigerate 30 minutes.

Pour over cream cheese mixture.

Refrigerate 4 hours or overnight.

Note: Each recipe indicates two cooking times.
The **first** is for a **650**-watt oven.
The **second** (in parentheses) is for an **800**-watt oven.

Fast and Fluffy Orange Pie

Preparation Time: 25 minutes
8 servings

Combine in 2-quart glass bowl:
4½ cups miniature marshmallows
¾ cup orange juice

Microwave uncovered on High for
2:30-3:30 (2:05-2:55) minutes, or until
marshmallows are melted, stirring twice
during cooking time.

If desired, stir in:
1 Tbsp. grated orange peel

Place in freezer 15-20 minutes, or until
slightly thickened, stirring once or twice.

Fold in:
8-oz. carton thawed frozen whipped
topping (about 3½ cups)

Spoon into:
9-inch prepared graham cracker crust

Refrigerate.

Quick Cherry Crunch

Preparation Time: 17 minutes
6-8 servings

Spread evenly in 8-inch square baking dish:
1 can cherry pie filling

Combine in bowl and sprinkle over pie
filling:
1 pkg. single-layer yellow cake mix
¼ cup chopped nuts, optional
2 Tbsp. brown sugar
2 tsp. cinnamon

Melt and pour over top:
½ cup butter, melted

Cover with waxed paper and microwave on
High for 12:00-14:00 (10:00-11:40) minutes,
or until topping is no longer doughy.

Note: Substitute fresh apples or any flavor pie
filling in place of cherry pie filling.

Note: Each recipe indicates two cooking times.
The **first** is for a **650**-watt oven.
The **second** (in parentheses) is for an **800**-watt oven.

Custards and Puddings — A Simple Process, An Excellent Result

- Stirring is needed only once or twice to eliminate lumps.
- There is no need to place custards in steaming water.
- Quick puddings may be cooked on High.
- Pies or large custards should be microwaved at 50-70%.
- Cook a custard for the shortest amount of suggested time. Then allow it to stand until set (it will appear very loose but should set during standing time). When the standing time is up, insert a knife into the center of the custard. If it comes out clean, it is done; if it does not, microwave the additional time suggested in the recipe.
- Sprinkle tops of finished puddings and custards with your favorite spice to create an appealing color.

A General Time Guideline

Food	Amount	Level	Time
Pudding mix	3¼ ozs.	High	6:00-7:00 (5:00-5:50) minutes
Egg Custard	3 ozs.	70%	6:00-7:00 (5:00-5:50) minutes
Tapioca	3¼ ozs.	High	6:00-7:00 (5:00-5:50) minutes

Note: Each recipe indicates two cooking times.
The **first** is for a **650**-watt oven.
The **second** (in parentheses) is for an **800**-watt oven.

Vanilla Pudding

Preparation Time: 5 minutes
2 servings

Combine in 2-quart measure:
- **1 cup milk**
- **1 egg**
- **1 Tbsp. cornstarch**
- **2 Tbsp. sugar**

Microwave on High for 45 (38) seconds. Stir. Microwave on High another 45 (38) seconds. Stir. Microwave on High again for 45 (38) seconds. Stir in:
- **¼ tsp. vanilla**
- **small pat butter**

Chill and serve with fruit.

Chocolate Pudding

Preparation Time: 5 minutes
2 servings

Combine in 2-quart measure:
- **1 cup milk**
- **1 square semi-sweet chocolate**
- **1 Tbsp. and 1 tsp. cornstarch**
- **2 Tbsp. sugar**

Microwave on High for 45 (38) seconds. Stir. Microwave on High another 45 (38) seconds. Stir. Microwave on High again for 45 (38) seconds. Stir in:
- **¼ tsp. vanilla**
- **small pat butter**

Chill and serve with whipped topping.

Rice Pudding

Preparation Time: 45 minutes
8-10 servings

Combine in 2-quart casserole:
- **4 cups milk**
- **1 cup uncooked regular rice**
- **½ cup sugar**
- **½ tsp. salt (optional)**

Cover and microwave on High for 9:00-10:00 (7:30-8:20) minutes. Microwave at 30% for 30-35 (25:00-29:10) minutes, or until liquid is absorbed.

Stir in:
- **2 Tbsp. butter**

Top with:
- **cinnamon or nutmeg**

Note: Each recipe indicates two cooking times.
The **first** is for a **650**-watt oven.
The **second** (in parentheses) is for an **800**-watt oven.

Instant Rice Pudding

Preparation Time: 11 minutes
8-10 servings

Combine in 2-quart glass measure:
3 cups milk
1 3/4 cups instant rice
2/3 cup sugar
2 Tbsp. cornstarch

Microwave on High for 3:00 (2:30) minutes.
Stir. Microwave on High 3:00 (2:30) more
minutes. Stir. Microwave on High an
additional 3:00 (2:30) minutes.

Stir in:
2 Tbsp. butter
1 tsp. vanilla

Piña Colada Rice Pudding

Preparation Time: 25 minutes
8 servings

Combine in 2-quart glass measure:
2 cups cooked rice
2 cups milk
1/4 cup cream of coconut or sugar
1/4 tsp. salt

Microwave on High for 15:00 (12:30)
minutes, stirring once. Add:
2 Tbsp. rum or 1 1/2 tsp. rum
flavoring

Set pudding aside.

Combine in 1-quart glass measure:
1 tsp. cornstarch
2 Tbsp. brown sugar
8-oz. can pineapple chunks with
juice

Microwave on High for 2:00 (1:40) minutes.
Stir. Microwave on High another 2:00 (1:40)
minutes. Stir in:
1 tsp. butter
2 Tbsp. rum or 1 1/2 tsp.
rum flavoring

Spoon pudding into serving dishes. Top
with pineapple sauce and:
1/4 cup toasted coconut

Note: Each recipe indicates two cooking times.
The **first** is for a **650**-watt oven.
The **second** (in parentheses) is for an **800**-watt oven.

Tapioca Pudding

Preparation Time: 12 minutes
8 servings

Combine in 2-quart measure:
2 cups milk
1/3 cup sugar
1/4 cup quick-cooking tapioca
1/4 tsp. salt
2 egg yolks, beaten

Microwave on High for 5:00-6:00 (4:10-5:00) minutes, stirring twice during that time.

Beat until frothy:
2 egg whites

Gradually beat in until stiff peaks form:
2 Tbsp. sugar

Fold egg whites into cooked pudding just until combined.

Note: For an interesting twist fold in 2 Tbsp. lemon or orange juice with egg whites.

Berry Fast Tapioca

Preparation Time: 7 minutes
6 servings

Combine in 2-quart glass bowl:
3 1/2-oz. pkg. tapioca pudding mix
1 cup water

Mix well. Microwave uncovered on High for 3:00-3:30 (2:30-2:55) minutes, or until mixture boils and thickens, stirring once. Set aside.

Microwave on High for 45-60 (38-50) seconds, or until partially thawed:
10-oz. pkg. frozen sweetened raspberries or strawberries

Add to hot pudding. Stir occasionally until thawed.

Fold in:
4-oz. carton frozen whipped topping (about 1 3/4 cups)

Refrigerate.

Note: Each recipe indicates two cooking times.
The **first** is for a **650**-watt oven.
The **second** (in parentheses) is for an **800**-watt oven.

Floating Island

Preparation Time: 15 minutes
6 servings

Combine in 4-cup glass measure:
   2/3 **cup sugar**
   1 **Tbsp. cornstarch**
   1/4 **tsp. salt**
   2 **cups milk**

Microwave on High for 4:00-6:00
(3:20-5:00) minutes, or until boiling.
Gradually stir into:
   3 **egg yolks, beaten**

Microwave on High for 2:00 (1:40) minutes,
stirring every 30 seconds.

Pour into shallow 1-quart casserole and chill
15 minutes.

In clean bowl beat until frothy:
   3 **egg whites**
   1/4 **tsp. cream of tartar, or salt**

Gradually add:
   1/3 **cup sugar**
   1/2 **tsp. vanilla**

Beat until stiff peaks form. Spoon onto
cooled custard. Microwave on High for
2:00 (1:40) minutes, until egg whites are set.
Serve warm or cold.

Vanilla Custard

Preparation Time: 12 minutes
6 servings

Combine in 2-quart glass measure:
   2/3 **cup sugar**
   2 1/2 **Tbsp. cornstarch**
   1 **Tbsp. flour**
   1/2 **tsp. salt**

Slowly stir in:
   3 **cups milk**

Microwave on High for 3:00 (2:30) minutes.
Stir. Microwave on High another 3:00 (2:30)
minutes. Stir. Microwave on High again for
3:00 (2:30) minutes. Slowly blend some of
the hot mixture into:
   3 **egg yolks, beaten**

When the temperature of the egg mixture
reaches that of the hot milk mixture,
combine the two mixtures gradually.
Microwave on High for 60 (50) seconds and
stir in:
   1 **Tbsp. butter**
   1 **tsp. vanilla**

Cover the surface with plastic wrap to
prevent skin from forming.

Note: Each recipe indicates two cooking times.
The **first** is for a **650**-watt oven.
The **second** (in parentheses) is for an **800**-watt oven.

Chocolate Custard

Preparation Time: 12 minutes
6 serving

Make Vanilla Custard recipe (see page 143).
During final step, stir in 1-1½ squares
melted unsweetened chocolate squares with
butter and vanilla.

Pumpkin Custard

Preparation Time: 25 minutes
6-8 servings

Microwave in 2-cup glass measure for
2:30 (2:05) minutes:
  1¾ cups milk

Blend in:
  4 eggs, beaten
  1 cup pumpkin, cooked
  ⅓ cup sugar
  1 tsp. vanilla
  ¼ tsp. salt

Sprinkle with:
  nutmeg

Microwave at 50% for 18:00-20:00
(15:00-16:40) minutes. Garnish with:
  whipped cream

Chocolate Mousse

Preparation Time: 6 minutes
6 servings

Measure into blender container:
  ¼ cup cold water
  1 envelope unflavored gelatin

Set aside.

Microwave on High for 60 (50) seconds:
  ¾ cup milk

Pour milk into blender and add:
  ¼ cup sugar
  ⅛ tsp. salt
  12 ozs. chocolate chips
  2 cups heavy cream
  1 tsp. vanilla
  1 egg
  6 Tbsp. rum (optional)
  2 ice cubes

Blend until smooth.

Pour into small sherbet glasses. Garnish
with:
  whipped cream
  chocolate shavings

Note: Each recipe indicates two cooking times.
The **first** is for a **650**-watt oven.
The **second** (in parentheses) is for an **800**-watt oven.

Vanilla Custard
Ice Cream

Preparation Time: 26 minutes
8 servings

Beat together in 4-cup glass measure:
2 cups milk
2 eggs
3/4 cup sugar

Microwave on High for 5:00-6:00 (4:10-5:00) minutes, stirring 2-3 times during that cooking time. Cool and blend in:
1 Tbsp. vanilla
1 cup whipping cream

Pour into ice cream freezer and process.

Chocolate Custard
Ice Cream

Preparation Time: 30 minutes
8 servings

Combine in 2-quart glass measure:
1/2 cup sugar
2 Tbsp. flour
1/4 tsp. salt

Beat in:
2 cups milk
2 eggs

Microwave uncovered on High for 6:00-7:00 (5:00-5:50) minutes, or until mixture starts to thicken. Stir 2-3 times during that cooking time to prevent lumps. Then stir in until melted:
4 ozs. sweet baking chocolate, broken into pieces

Cool.

Stir in:
2 cups heavy cream
1 1/2 tsp. vanilla

Add, if desired:
1 cup shredded coconut
1 cup chopped pecans

Process in ice cream freezer according to manufacturer's directions.

Note: Each recipe indicates two cooking times. The **first** is for a **650**-watt oven. The **second** (in parentheses) is for an **800**-watt oven.

Individual Cheesecakes

Preparation Time: 15 minutes
Yields 24 cakes

Microwave on High for 1:00-2:00 (50 seconds-1:40) minutes in glass mixing bowl until softened:
2 8-oz. pkgs. cream cheese

Beat until smooth, then blend in the following one at a time:
¾ cup sugar
2 eggs
1 Tbsp. lemon juice
1 tsp. vanilla

Microwave on High for 4:00-5:00 (3:20-4:10) minutes, or until thickened. Stir occasionally.

Beat until smooth and set aside.

Line 24 muffin cups with paper liners and place in each:
1 vanilla wafer

Top each with:
reserved cream cheese filling
a dollop of preserves, jelly,
    or pie filling

Refrigerate or freeze.

Bread Pudding

Preparation Time: 15 minutes
8 servings

Place in 9-inch round baking dish:
6 slices bread, cubed

Combine in 4-cup glass measure and microwave on High for 3:00 (2:30) minutes:
2 cups milk
1 Tbsp. butter

Stir in:
3 eggs, beaten
1 cup sugar
½ tsp. cinnamon
¼ tsp. salt
1 tsp. vanilla
½ cup raisins

Pour over bread cubes. Microwave on High for 7:00-9:00 (5:50-7:30) minutes.

Note: Each recipe indicates two cooking times.
The **first** is for a **650**-watt oven.
The **second** (in parentheses) is for an **800**-watt oven.

Chocolate Bread Pudding

Preparation Time: 20 minutes
8 servings

Combine in glass loaf pan:
3 cups bread cubes
1/4 cup sugar
1 tsp. cinnamon
1/2 tsp. nutmeg
1/2 cup chopped nuts

Microwave on High for 2:00 (1:40) minutes
in 4-cup glass measure:
1 1/2 cups milk
2 squares semi-sweet chocolate

Blend in:
1/2 cup sugar
3 eggs
1 tsp. vanilla

Pour over bread cubes. Microwave on High
for 9:00-11:00 (7:30-9:10) minutes.

Note: Each recipe indicates two cooking times.
The **first** is for a **650**-watt oven.
The **second** (in parentheses) is for an **800**-watt oven.

Notes

Note: Each recipe indicates two cooking times.
The **first** is for a **650**-watt oven.
The **second** (in parentheses) is for an **800**-watt oven.

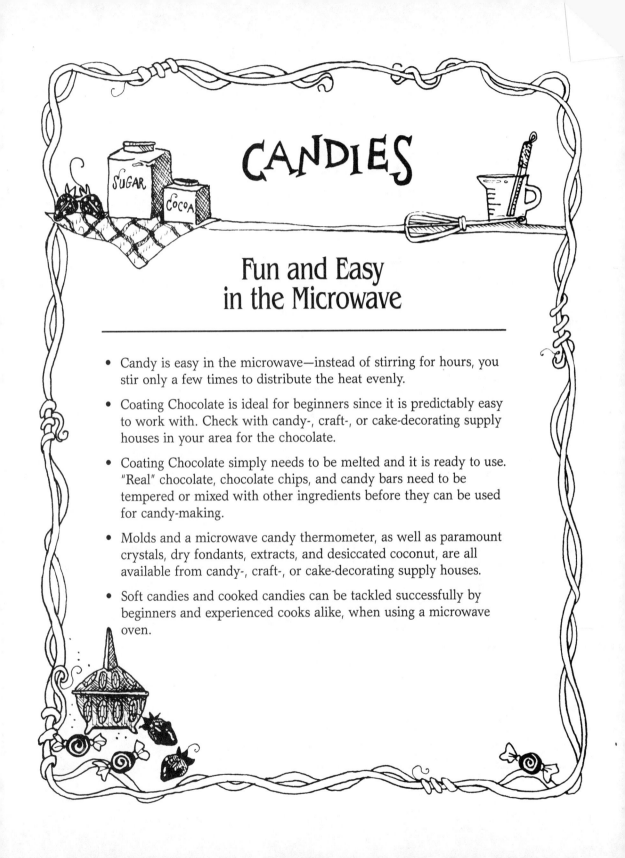

CANDIES

Fun and Easy
in the Microwave

- Candy is easy in the microwave—instead of stirring for hours, you stir only a few times to distribute the heat evenly.

- Coating Chocolate is ideal for beginners since it is predictably easy to work with. Check with candy-, craft-, or cake-decorating supply houses in your area for the chocolate.

- Coating Chocolate simply needs to be melted and it is ready to use. "Real" chocolate, chocolate chips, and candy bars need to be tempered or mixed with other ingredients before they can be used for candy-making.

- Molds and a microwave candy thermometer, as well as paramount crystals, dry fondants, extracts, and desiccated coconut, are all available from candy-, craft-, or cake-decorating supply houses.

- Soft candies and cooked candies can be tackled successfully by beginners and experienced cooks alike, when using a microwave oven.

- Use a microwave candy thermometer. (The traditional cold water test can be used, but is not as accurate as a thermometer.)

Candy Stage	Temperature	Cold water test
Soft ball	235°-240°F	Forms a ball, but flattens when taken out of water
Firm ball	245°-250°F	Holds shape until pressed
Hard ball	255°-265°F	Holds its shape but is pliable
Soft crack	270°-290°F	Separates into threads
Hard crack	300°-310°F	Forms hard, brittle threads

- Use a glass measure with a handle. Candies are hot, and round bowls are very difficult to handle. Measuring cups that are deep work better than shallow ones.

- Cover the glass measure with plastic wrap. The steam that is created dissolves the sugar that forms on the sides of the bowl. Be sure to stir the candy and scrape the sides of the bowl to keep all sugar dissolved.

- Avoid making candy on humid days. High altitude also affects the temperature. Check the temperature necessary to boil water in your home on the day you choose to make candy, then calculate the difference between that temperature and 212°F. Add or subtract that amount to the temperature(s) designated in the recipe you are using.

- Keep a constant check on the temperature of the candy while it is cooking. It may seem to take a long time until you notice a temperature change, but once it reaches 220°F it will rise quickly.

- Use a container large enough to handle the mixture. Boil-over often occurs with products containing milk and butter.

- When adding baking soda after microwaving, allow the mixture to stand for 2-3 minutes. The hot temperatures will not allow the baking soda to work to its full potential.

Easy Chocolate Chip Fudge

Preparation Time: 5 minutes
Yields 48 pieces

Combine in 8-cup glass bowl:
1 can sweetened condensed milk
(or use recipe below)
12 ozs. chocolate chips

Microwave on High for 1:00-1:30
(50 seconds-1:15) minutes, or until chips
melt when stirred (about 100°F).

Stir in:
½ cup chopped nuts
1 tsp. vanilla

Pour into buttered 8-inch square pan.

Sweetened Condensed Milk

Preparation Time: 5 minutes
Yields 14 ounces

Combine in 4-cup glass measure:
1½ cups sugar
⅔ cup water
½ cup butter

Microwave on High for 60 (50) seconds. Stir.
Microwave on High another 60 (50)
seconds. Stir. Microwave on High again for
60 (50) seconds and then stir. Continue until
mixture boils.

Combine in blender with:
2 cups dry milk

Process until smooth.

Peanut Butter Fudge

Preparation Time: 5 minutes
Yields 48 pieces

Combine in 8-cup glass bowl:
1 can sweetened condensed milk
(or use recipe at left)
12 ozs. peanut butter chips

Microwave on High for 1:00-1:30
(50 seconds-1:15) minutes, or until chips
melt when stirred (about 100°F).

Stir in:
½ cup chopped peanuts
1 tsp. vanilla

Pour into buttered 8-inch square pan.

Note: Each recipe indicates two cooking times.
The **first** is for a **650**-watt oven.
The **second** (in parentheses) is for an **800**-watt oven.

Butterscotch Fudge

Preparation Time: 5 minutes
Yields 48 pieces

Combine in 8-inch glass bowl:
1 can sweetened condensed milk
(or use recipe on page 151)
12 ozs. butterscotch chips

Microwave on High for 1:00-1:30
(50 seconds-1:15) minutes, or until chips
melt when stirred (about 100°F).

Stir in:
1 tsp. vanilla

Pour into buttered 8-inch square pan.

Vanilla Fudge

Preparation Time: 5 minutes
Yields 48 pieces

Combine in 8-cup glass bowl:
1 can sweetened condensed milk
(or use recipe on page 151)
12 ozs. white chocolate chips
(available at supply stores)

Microwave on High for 1:00-1:30
(50 seconds-1:15) minutes, or until chips
melt when stirred (about 100°F).

Stir in:
½ cup chopped nuts
1 tsp. vanilla

Pour into buttered 8-inch square pan.

Note: Each recipe indicates two cooking times.
The **first** is for a **650**-watt oven.
The **second** (in parentheses) is for an **800**-watt oven.

Special Fudge Sauce

Preparation Time: 8 minutes
Yields 2½ cups

Combine and microwave on High for 6:00-7:00 (5:00-5:50) minutes until bubbly:
2 cups brown sugar
⅔ cup corn syrup
⅓ cup cocoa powder
½ cup light cream

Stir in:
1 tsp. vanilla

Serve warm over ice cream.

Melting Coatings

Place in 4-cup glass measure:
1 lb. coating wafers or pieces

Microwave on High for 2:00 (1:40) minutes. Stir. Microwave on High for 60 (50) seconds. Stir. Microwave on High in 30 (25)-second intervals until chocolate is smooth when stirred.

Note: Be sure to stir. Chocolate may retain its shape but still be melted. Do not overcook; the chocolate can be ruined.

Dipping Chocolates

To dip chocolates, melt the coating as directed at left. Prepare your favorite centers (ideas listed below) and dip them into coatings.

• Dried and fresh fruits work well (if you use fresh fruits, be sure they are clean and dry before dipping): strawberries, apple slices, apricots, raisins, pineapple chunks, banana slices.

• Dry finger foods: sugar wafers, round crackers sandwiched with peanut butter, pretzels, potato chips, animal crackers, any cookies, nuts.

Note: Each recipe indicates two cooking times. The **first** is for a **650**-watt oven. The **second** (in parentheses) is for an **800**-watt oven.

Molded Candies

To mold candies, pour melted coating chocolate into molds. Tap molds until all the air bubbles come to the top and then burst. Chill until candies fall out of the molds when tapped gently. The time will vary with the molds (larger molds take more time); for an average-sized mold, 10 to 15 minutes in the freezer should be enough. Unmold on a clean kitchen towel to avoid breakage.

For ease in filling molds, plastic squeeze bottles work well. Pour the melted chocolate into a clean, dry, thin plastic squeeze bottle. Its lid may need to be trimmed to allow the coating to flow easily. Squeeze until each mold is full. When the bottle is empty, place it in the freezer for a few minutes, then squeeze and shake out the hardened coating. These chips can be added to the next batch or eaten!

Clusters and Barks

Clusters are made by adding dry ingredients to melted coating chocolate, which is then spooned onto waxed paper and cooled until set.

Barks are made by adding dry ingredients to melted coating chocolate which is then spread onto waxed paper and cooled until set. These are then broken into pieces.

Barks and clusters are usually made with dry ingredients of small pieces: nuts, raisins, coconut, broken pretzels, Chinese noodles, cereals, and anything else you would like covered with chocolate.

Rocky Road

Preparation Time: 15 minutes

Combine in 2-quart glass measure:
1 lb. milk chocolate coating
1 cup peanut butter

Microwave on High for 3:00-5:00 (2:30-4:10) minutes, or until soft.

Stir until smooth. Stir into chocolate to coat:
1 lb. miniature marshmallows
1 lb. salted peanuts

Note: Each recipe indicates two cooking times.
The **first** is for a **650**-watt oven.
The **second** (in parentheses) is for an **800**-watt oven.

Spread on waxed paper or drop by spoonfuls onto waxed paper. Allow to set.

Tiger Butter

Preparation Time: 15 minutes

Microwave on High for 2:00 (1:40) minutes:
2 lbs. white coating chocolate
4 Tbsp. paramount crystals
1 cup peanut butter

Stir. Microwave on High for 2:00 (1:40) more minutes. Stir. Microwave on High for 60 (50) seconds, or until mixture is smooth when stirred.

Spread on a waxed paper-lined cookie sheet and top with:
1 cup melted milk chocolate

Marble by swirling scraper through the mixture. Cut into squares when set.

Chocolate Leather

In 4-cup glass measure, microwave on High for 3:00 (2:30) minutes:
1 cup light corn syrup

Stir in:
2 cups chocolate pieces

Pour onto waxed paper.

Allow to set up 4 hours or overnight.

Roll or shape as desired.

Zebra Butter

Preparation Time: 15 minutes

Microwave on High for 2:00 (1:40) minutes:
2 lbs. white coating chocolate
4 Tbsp. paramount crystals
1 cup desiccated coconut (dried)

Stir. Microwave on High for 2:00 (1:40) more minutes. Stir. Microwave on High for 60 (50) seconds, or until mixture is smooth when stirred.

Spread on a waxed paper-lined cookie sheet and top with:
1 cup melted dark chocolate

Marble by swirling scraper through the mixture. Cut into squares when set.

Note: Each recipe indicates two cooking times. The **first** is for a **650**-watt oven. The **second** (in parentheses) is for an **800**-watt oven.

Chocolate Swirl

Preparation Time: 15 minutes

Microwave on High for 2:00 (1:40) minutes:
2 lbs. milk chocolate coating wafers
4 Tbsp. paramount crystals

Stir. Microwave on High for 2:00 (1:40) more minutes. Stir. Microwave on High for 60 (50) seconds, or until mixture is smooth when stirred.

Spread on a waxed paper-lined cookie sheet and top with:
1 cup melted dark chocolate

Marble by swirling scraper through the mixture. Cut into squares when set.

Layered Mints

Preparation Time: 15 minutes

Microwave on High for 2:00 (1:40) minutes:
2 lbs. dark chocolate coating wafers
4 Tbsp. paramount crystals

Stir. Microwave on High for 2:00 (1:40) more minutes. Stir. Microwave on High for 60 (50) seconds, or until mixture is smooth when stirred.

Spread on a waxed paper-lined cookie sheet. Allow to set and top with:
1 cup melted dark chocolate

Then follow the instructions for Mint Swirl (below), spreading the green mixture on top of the melted chocolate above. Do NOT marble. Repeat Mint Swirl directions again, adding another layer to the already prepared layers. Do NOT marble. Cut into squares when set.

Mint Swirl

Preparation Time: 15 minutes

Microwave on High for 2:00 (1:40) minutes:
2 lbs. green coating wafers
4 Tbsp. paramount crystals

Stir. Microwave on High for 2:00 (1:40) more minutes. Stir. Microwave on High for 60 (50) seconds, or until mixture is smooth when stirred.

Stir in:
6-8 drops peppermint oil

Spread on a waxed paper-lined cookie sheet and top with:
1 cup melted chocolate

Marble by swirling scraper through the mixture. Cut into squares when set.

Note: Oils are available through candy supply houses or most pharmacies. Do not use extracts which will ruin your coating.

Note: Each recipe indicates two cooking times.
The **first** is for a 650-watt oven.
The **second** (in parentheses) is for an 800-watt oven.

Silky Way

Combine in glass measuring cup:
1 cup marshmallow creme (7-oz. jar)
1/2 cup melted dark coating chocolate (see Melting Coatings, page 153)

Pour into buttered 8-inch square pan. Allow to set and cut into squares. Dip in melted milk chocolate.

Moist Coconut Centers

Microwave on High for 60 (50) seconds, or until boiling:
1 cup light corn syrup

Stir in:
1/2 lb. desiccated coconut (dry)
1/2 tsp. coconut extract

Easy Cream Centers for Dipping or Eating

Preparation Time: 5 minutes

Microwave on High for 60 (50) seconds:
2 Tbsp. butter
6 Tbsp. heavy cream

Stir in:
1 lb. dry fondant

Knead by hand until smooth and creamy.

Note: This is a basic mixture and can be used as above or colored and flavored as desired:
Chocolate—knead in melted chocolate squares
Mint—add a few drops peppermint and a few drops red or green food coloring
Nut—knead in finely chopped nuts
Fruit and nut—knead in candied fruit and ground nuts

Try your own concoctions. The texture and consistency of this mixture can be altered by the amount of fondant used.

Note: Each recipe indicates two cooking times. The **first** is for a **650**-watt oven. The **second** (in parentheses) is for an **800**-watt oven.

Peanut Butter Centers

Combine in mixer bowl:
2 cups peanut butter
¼ cup margarine or butter
1 lb. confectioners' sugar
1 tsp. vanilla

Shape into balls and dip in melted milk chocolate coating (see Melting Coatings, page 153).

Caramel Krispies

Combine in mixing bowl:
½ lb. caramel, melted
1½ cups crisp rice cereal

Pack into greased 8-inch square pan. Allow to set and cut into squares. Dip in melted milk chocolate coating (see Melting Coatings, page 153).

Turtles

Arrange nuts in clusters on buttered waxed paper:
¼ lb. pecans, cashews, or almonds

Top each cluster with:
dab of melted chocolate coating
(see Melting Coatings, page 153)

Top each cluster with:
caramel, about ¼ lb. in all

Top each cluster with:
melted coating of your choice, being sure to cover caramel

Allow to cool until set.

Jellies

Preparation Time: 1 hour
Yields 60 pieces

Microwave on High for 3:00 (2:30) minutes in 4-cup glass measure:
1 cup water

Stir in:
.6-oz. pkg. flavored gelatin
2 envelopes unflavored gelatin
1 cup cold water

Stir until dissolved. Pour into greased 9 x 13 baking pan. Chill until firm. Cut into squares. Eat as is or dip in chocolate coating (see Melting Coatings, page 153).

Note: Each recipe indicates two cooking times.
The **first** is for a **650**-watt oven.
The **second** (in parentheses) is for an **800**-watt oven.

Nutty Bars

Preparation Time: 30 minutes
Yields 60 pieces

Microwave in 2-quart glass measure for
4:00 (3:20) minutes:
4 cups dry quick rolled oats
1/2 cup margarine

Stir in and microwave on High for 2:00
(1:40) minutes:
1 cup brown sugar
1/2 cup corn syrup

Pour into greased 9 x 13 baking pan. Top
with the following chocolate mixture.

Combine in 2-cup measure and microwave
on High for 60 (50) seconds, or until melted:
2/3 cup chocolate chips
1/4 cup peanut butter

Allow bars to set and cut into squares.

Crispy Bars

Preparation Time: 30 minutes
Yields 48 bars

Combine in 3-quart glass casserole and
microwave on High for 3:00 (2:30) minutes:
1/4 cup margarine or butter
5 cups mini-marshmallows or 40
large marshmallows

Stir until smooth and then stir in:
5 cups crisp rice cereal

Press mixture into buttered 9 x 13 baking
pan. Chill and cut into squares.

Note: Each recipe indicates two cooking times.
The **first** is for a **650**-watt oven.
The **second** (in parentheses) is for an **800**-watt oven.

Peanut Crispy Bars

Preparation Time: 30 minutes
Yields 48 bars

Combine in 3-quart glass casserole and microwave on High for 3:00 (2:30) minutes:
  ¼ cup margarine or butter
  5 cups mini-marshmallows or 40 large marshmallows
  ⅓ cup peanut butter

Stir until smooth and then stir in:
  5 cups crisp rice cereal
  1 cup peanuts

Press mixture into buttered 9 x 13 baking pan. Chill and cut into squares.

Dip each in milk chocolate coating (see Melting Coatings, page 153).

Truffles

Preparation Time: 1½ hours

Combine in 2-quart glass measure:
  1 cup heavy cream
  1 lb. plus 6 ozs. semi-sweet chocolate, chopped

Microwave on High for 2:00 (1:40) minutes. Stir until smooth. Cool. Drop by teaspoonfuls onto waxed paper. Refrigerate 1 hour. Roll into balls. Dip in coating chocolate or roll in nuts (see Melting Coatings, page 153).

Cordial Truffles

Preparation Time: 1½ hours

Combine in 2-quart glass measure:
  1 cup heavy cream
  1 lb. plus 6 ozs. semi-sweet chocolate, chopped
  3 Tbsp. Kirschwasser, rum, or cherry juice

Microwave on High for 2:00 (1:40) minutes. Stir until smooth. Cool. Drop by teaspoonfuls onto waxed paper. Refrigerate 1 hour. Roll into balls. Dip in coating chocolate (see Melting Coatings, page 153) or roll in nuts.

Note: Each recipe indicates two cooking times.
The **first** is for a **650**-watt oven.
The **second** (in parentheses) is for an **800**-watt oven.

Cherry Cordials

Preparation Time: 30 minutes
Yields 24 pieces

Drain and then soak in Kirschwasser or brandy, if desired, overnight:
1 jar maraschino cherries

Combine and microwave on High for 30 (25) seconds:
½ cup dry fondant
3 Tbsp. maraschino cherry juice, from soaked cherries

Line cordial molds with melted dark coating chocolate (see Melting Coatings, page 153). Dot with cherry juice mixture. Add to each mold maraschino cherries, drained, and dried. Seal with melted dark chocolate coating.

Peanut Brittle

Preparation Time: 20 minutes

Combine in 2-quart glass measure and microwave on High for 5:00 (4:10) minutes:
1½ cups sugar
½ cup light corn syrup
½ cup water
dash salt

Stir and then microwave on High for 13:00-15:00 (10:50-12:30) minutes, or to 300°F. Allow to stand 2 minutes and then stir in:
2 cups peanuts
1 Tbsp. butter
1 tsp. baking soda
1 tsp. vanilla

Pour onto buttered cookie sheet. Cool and break into pieces.

Almond Butter Crunch

Preparation Time: 12 minutes

Combine in 2-quart glass measure and microwave on High for 12:00 (10:00) minutes, or to 300°F.
1 cup butter
1⅓ cups granulated sugar
1 Tbsp. corn syrup
3 Tbsp. water

Stir in:
1 cup almonds, chopped

Pour onto buttered cookie sheet. Cool and break into pieces.

Note: Each recipe indicates two cooking times. The **first** is for a 650-watt oven. The **second** (in parentheses) is for an 800-watt oven.

Peanut Butter Fingers

Preparation Time: 15 minutes

Combine in 2-quart glass measure and microwave on High to 310°F.
1 cup granulated sugar
1/3 cup corn syrup
1/3 cup water

Stir in:
1 cup peanut butter

Spread to desired thickness on buttered cookie sheet. Score with knife or pastry wheel. Break apart when cool.

Toffee

Preparation Time: 10 minutes

Combine in 2-quart glass measure and microwave on High for 4:00 (3:20) minutes:
1 cup butter
1 1/3 cups sugar
1 Tbsp. light corn syrup
2 Tbsp. water

Stir. Microwave on High for 6:00-8:00 (5:00-6:40) minutes or to 300°F. Stir in:
1 tsp. vanilla
1/3 cup finely chopped nuts

Pour onto buttered cookie sheet and score with knife or pastry wheel.

Top with:
1/2 cup chocolate pieces, melted
1/4 cup finely chopped nuts

Chill and break into pieces.

Caramel Corn

Preparation Time: 7 minutes

Combine in 2-quart glass measure and microwave on High for 3:00 (2:30) minutes, or to boiling:
1 cup brown sugar
1/2 cup butter
1/4 cup light corn syrup
1/2 tsp. salt

Microwave at 30% for 4:00 (3:20) minutes. Let stand 2 minutes and stir in:
1/2 tsp. baking soda
2/3 cup chopped nuts

Pour over:
4 qts. popped popcorn (16 cups)

Mix until popcorn is coated and nuts are well distributed.

Note: Each recipe indicates two cooking times.
The **first** is for a **650**-watt oven.
The **second** (in parentheses) is for an **800**-watt oven.

Caramels

Preparation Time: 20 minutes

Combine in 2-quart glass measure and microwave on High for 8:00 (6:40) minutes, or until boiling:

1 cup granulated sugar
1 cup dark corn syrup
1 cup heavy cream
¼ cup butter

Stir well and microwave on High for 10:00 (8:20) more minutes, or until temperature reaches 250°F, stirring often. Pour into buttered 11 x 7 baking pan. Chill and cut into squares.

Note: 1 cup chopped nuts can be stirred in before pouring mixture into buttered pan.

Big Batch Caramels

Preparation Time: 1 hour

Microwave in 4-quart bowl on High for 60 (50) seconds:

1 cup butter

Stir in:

2 cups sugar
2 cups light corn syrup
1 cup heavy cream

Microwave on High for 24:00 (20:00) minutes. Stir in:

1 cup heavy cream

Insert candy thermometer and cook to 245°F. Stir in:

1 Tbsp. vanilla

Pour into buttered 9 x 13 pan. Cool. Cut into squares.

Sponge Candy

Preparation Time: 10 minutes

Combine in 2-quart glass measure and microwave on High for 8:00-10:00 (6:40-8:20) minutes, or until temperature reaches 300°F.
   1 cup granulated sugar
   1 cup light corn syrup

Allow to stand 2 minutes. Stir in:
   4 tsp. baking soda
   1 tsp. maple flavoring

Spread onto buttered baking sheet. Chill and break into pieces, which may be dipped in chocolate (see Melting Coatings, page 153).

Hard Candies

Preparation Time: 6 minutes

Combine in 2-quart glass measure and microwave on High for 6:00 (5:00) minutes, or until mixture comes to a full boil:
   2 cups granulated sugar
   ⅓ cup water
   ½ cup corn syrup

Stir well and continue to microwave on High for 8:00 (6:40) minutes, or until temperature reaches 300°F. Pour into buttered hard candy molds or onto buttered cookie sheet. Score with sharp knife or pastry wheel. Chill and break apart.

Note: Each recipe indicates two cooking times.
The **first** is for a **650**-watt oven.
The **second** (in parentheses) is for an **800**-watt oven.

APPETIZERS AND BEVERAGES

Bacon Appetizers

Arrange on paper towel:
  **1 lb. bacon slices cut in half
  lengthwise**

Place paper towel on meat rack or paper plate. Cover with another paper towel. Microwave on High for 4:00-5:00 (3:20-4:10) minutes. Assemble favorite fillings:
  **water chestnuts
  pineapple chunks
  pretzel nuggets
  fish nuggets
  vegetable nuggets
  hot dog chunks
  liverwurst
  cheese chunks
  bread
  chicken livers, cut in pieces
  apple chunks
  mushrooms
  shrimp
  lobster
  olives**

Wrap bacon slices around filling pieces. Secure with wooden picks. Place on fresh paper towel, either on the rack or on a paper plate. Cover with another paper towel. Microwave on High for 6:00-7:00 (5:00-5:50) minutes, or until bacon is crisp.

Butterflied Wieners

Preparation Time: 6 minutes
8 servings

Prepare:
  1 lb. jumbo hot dogs

by cutting each wiener crosswise into 3 pieces. Then cut each piece in half lengthwise to make 6 pieces. Slit each piece through its ends leaving a 1/4-inch join in center. Set aside.

Mix in 1½-quart casserole:
  **¼ cup honey
  1 bottle barbecue sauce**

Cover and microwave on High for 60 (50) seconds. Stir. Add hot dogs. Microwave on High for 3:00 (2:30) minutes or until ends curl. Serve with toothpicks.

Note: Each recipe indicates two cooking times.
The **first** is for a **650**-watt oven.
The **second** (in parentheses) is for an **800**-watt oven.

Spicy Stuffed Mushrooms

Preparation Time: 20 minutes
Yields 20-24 mushrooms

Microwave on High for 4:00 (3:20) minutes:
1 lb. Italian sausage, loose

Stir in:
2 Tbsp. catsup
1/8 tsp. oregano
dash garlic powder

Microwave on High for 60 (50) seconds.

Fill:
20-24 mushroom caps

Top with:
mozzarella cheese, grated
fresh parsley

Microwave on High for 2:00-3:00
(1:40-2:30) minutes, until caps are warm
and cheese is melted.

Ham Roll-Ups

Preparation Time: 5 minutes

Layer:
cooked ham slices
swiss cheese slices

Top with:
cranberry-orange relish

Roll and slice each roll into 4 pieces. Secure
with toothpicks. Microwave at 80% until
cheese begins to melt. Serve warm.

Note: Each recipe indicates two cooking times.
The **first** is for a **650**-watt oven.
The **second** (in parentheses) is for an **800**-watt oven.

Light Vegetable Dip

Preparation Time: 15 minutes
Yields 2½ cups

Pierce and microwave on High for
6:00-7:00 (5:00-5:50) minutes:
1 eggplant (about 1 pound)

Set aside to cool.

Combine in small bowl:
1 small onion, minced
½ bell pepper, minced
1 clove garlic, minced
1 tsp. lemon juice
½ tsp. salt
⅛ tsp. pepper

Microwave on High for 2:00 (1:40) minutes,
or until vegetables are limp. Place vegetable
mixture in blender with:
1 cup plain yogurt

Add pulp scooped from eggplant and blend
until mixed well. Cover and chill
thoroughly. Serve with antipasto.

Light Fruit Salad

Preparation Time: 20 minutes
4 servings

Drain **juice** from 8-oz. can unsweetened
pineapple chunks into 2-cup glass measure
and mix with the following ingredients until
smooth:
1 Tbsp. lemon juice
1 egg, beaten
1½ tsp. cornstarch

Microwave on High for 3:00 (2:30) minutes,
or until mixture thickens and boils, stirring
twice during cooking time. Chill about 15
minutes, then mix in:
⅓ cup plain yogurt

Pour over:
1 apple, cut into chunks
1 banana, sliced
1 orange, sectioned and cut
pineapple chunks

Note: Each recipe indicates two cooking times.
The **first** is for a **650**-watt oven.
The **second** (in parentheses) is for an **800**-watt oven.

Cream Cheese Fruit Spread

Preparation Time: 2 minutes
Yields 1 cup

Place in 1-quart glass bowl:
8-oz. pkg. cream cheese

Microwave uncovered on High for 45-60 (38-50) seconds, or until softened.

Stir in:
¼-½ cup dried fruit and raisin mixture, diced
2 Tbsp. brown sugar
¼ tsp. cinnamon

If desired, add 2 Tbsp. chopped nuts with fruit. Store leftover spread in refrigerator. For ease in spreading, microwave on High for 30-60 (25-50) seconds, stirring once.

Peppermint Tea

Use pieces of candy cane with regular tea for a minty taste and sweetness.

Boiling Water in a Cup

Microwave on High for 2:30-3:00 (2:05-2:30) minutes:
1 cup water in 10-ounce mug

Microwave on High for 4:30-5:30 (3:45-4:35) minutes:
1 cup water in each of 2 10-ounce mugs

When water boils, stir in instant hot drink mix or soup.

Spiced Cider

Preparation Time: 8 minutes
Yields 1 quart

Mix in microwave-safe 2-quart container:
1 quart apple cider
¼ cup light brown sugar
½ tsp. whole cloves
½ tsp. whole allspice
1 cinnamon stick
dash salt

Microwave on High for 6:00 (5:00) minutes.

Note: Each recipe indicates two cooking times. The **first** is for a **650**-watt oven. The **second** (in parentheses) is for an **800**-watt oven.

Frozen Orange Drink

Combine the following in a blender:
2 cups milk
**6-oz. can frozen concentrated orange
    juice**
1 egg
1 Tbsp. sugar
1 tsp. vanilla
6 ice cubes, partially crushed

Hot Chocolate
from Scratch

Preparation Time: 8 minutes
2 servings

Blend together in small bowl:
2 Tbsp. unsweetened cocoa powder
2 Tbsp. sugar
2 Tbsp. hot water

Cover and microwave on High for 60 (50)
seconds.

Stir in:
1¾ cups milk

Cover and microwave on High for
3:30 4:30 (2:55 3:45) minutes, stirring 3
times during that cooking time.

Stir in:
¼ tsp. vanilla

Dip mixture into 2 10-oz. microwave-safe
mugs. Top each with a marshmallow, if
desired, then microwave on High for
60 (50) seconds.

Note: Each recipe indicates two cooking times.
The **first** is for a **650**-watt oven.
The **second** (in parentheses) is for an **800**-watt oven.

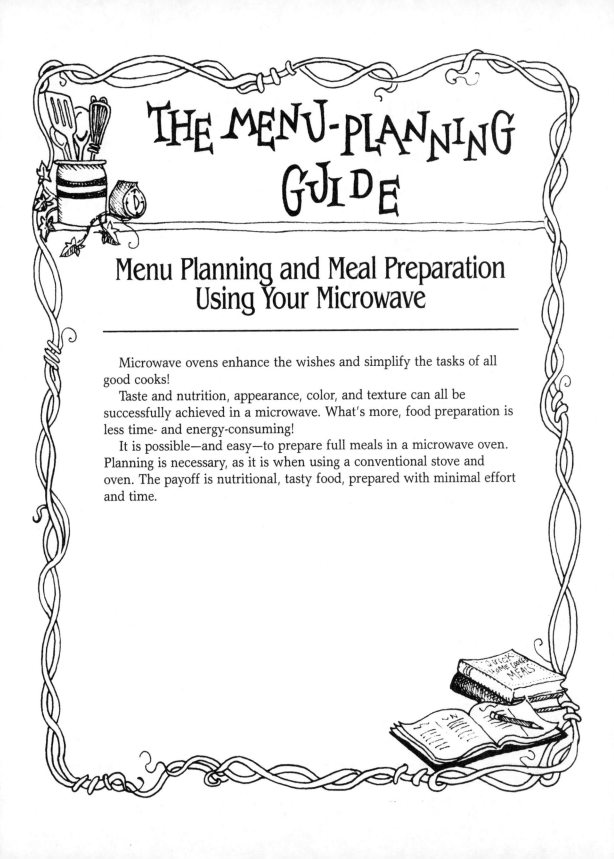

THE MENU-PLANNING GUIDE

Menu Planning and Meal Preparation Using Your Microwave

Microwave ovens enhance the wishes and simplify the tasks of all good cooks!

Taste and nutrition, appearance, color, and texture can all be successfully achieved in a microwave. What's more, food preparation is less time- and energy-consuming!

It is possible—and easy—to prepare full meals in a microwave oven. Planning is necessary, as it is when using a conventional stove and oven. The payoff is nutritional, tasty food, prepared with minimal effort and time.

Making Meals in a Microwave

There are several ways to maximize your microwave's capacity in meal preparation. Here are particular methods that work well:

- Prepare meals ahead of time so they can be microwaved in minutes at mealtime. Then organize those meals in your refrigerator or freezer so that their cooking times correspond to the time intervals you have available. A blue label could indicate a 4-minute preparation; a white label an 8-minute preparation; a red label a 12-minute preparation, and so on.

- Fix casseroles when you have time, then freeze them so they're available for reheating when you're short on time.

    1. Although large-quantity casseroles may require nearly as much time in a microwave as in a conventional oven, there are certain advantages to using a microwave in their preparation. As with other foods, nutrients are better retained. In addition, preparation and cleanup are quick and easy because of using one dish for all steps.

    2. Although precooking of certain elements may be necessary, some of that can be done with considerable time-saving in the microwave. For example, chopped onions or peppers can be precooked quickly in the same dish in which the casserole will be cooked and served.

    3. In some cases, pasta or rice need not be precooked (see Lasagna recipe, page 66); the noodles can be cooked in their dehydrated form. If the recipe calls for pasta or rice to be cooked, you may save that step by adding extra liquid (2 Tbsp. per ounce), and by cooking the casserole longer (add 1 minute per 2 ozs. of dehydrated pasta or rice).

    4. Leftovers can be frozen and reheated in single- or multiple-portion sizes. Because of the cooking method, these extras don't have a "leftover" taste, and they remain moist and flavorful when properly covered and reheated.

- Program your microwave so your meal is prepared when you expect to arrive home.

- Plan a meal with various dishes, microwaving according to each food's cooking and standing time.

    1. Foods that take longer to cook usually have a longer standing time. Cook those foods first because they will also hold their heat a proportionately longer time.

    Foods that have a high content of water, sugar, or fat usually hold their cooking temperatures well.

    2. Foods with shorter cooking times should be cooked last because they can be cooked during the other food's standing time.

    3. Foods with similar cooking times can usually be cooked at the same time; add their cooking times together to calculate the total cooking time needed.

4. A sample meal— Microwave a 3-lb. chicken for 20 minutes. Remove from oven. Let stand 10-12 minutes.

Next, microwave 4 baked potatoes for 12 minutes. Remove from oven. Let stand 4-5 minutes.

Finally, microwave 10-oz. pkg. of vegetables for 4 minutes.

Serve chicken, potatoes, and vegetables with tossed salad and rolls, and cherry crunch (prepared earlier) for dessert.

- Do Meal-in-One cooking. It is possible, if your oven is large enough, to cook several dishes at a time in your microwave. To determine whether this method is a good one for the menu you have chosen, consider these basic guidelines:

    1. If all the foods you are preparing take less than 15 minutes each, add their cooking times together and microwave all at once.

    2. If all the foods require between 15 and 35 minutes each, add their cooking times together, then subtract 5 minutes to arrive at the right amount of time needed for cooking all foods in the oven at once.

    3. If any one food takes more than 35 minutes, all other foods can be cooked during that one food's cooking time. (Add or remove dishes as needed while cooking.)

If you prepare more than one dish at a time in your microwave, remember this:

1. Use the oven's rack only when there is not enough room for all the dishes to sit on the floor of the oven. Remove the rack if it is not needed.

2. Since foods on the rack receive and absorb the microwaves first, place foods there that require longer cooking time. For example, spare ribs and potatoes would be set on the rack, while corn would be placed on the floor of the oven. Or pork chops and potatoes would be positioned on the rack and boxed vegetables on the bottom of the oven.

3. If all foods can be placed in the oven at once and have similar cooking times, reverse the dishes halfway through the cooking, moving those on the rack to the floor and those on the bottom to the rack.

4. When possible, stagger the dishes, so that those on the rack are not directly above those on the oven floor.

5. Use High whenever you cook more than one food at a time.

6. Browning dishes and crispers cannot be used when more than one item is being cooked or when the rack is being used.

7. Foods that cook very quickly, such as breads that are being reheated, should be done separately.

Menu Suggestions and Procedures
for Meals in the Microwave

Meat Loaf
Scalloped Potatoes
Vegetable
Chocolate Pudding

Preparation Time: 25 minutes
4 servings

1. Prepare Chocolate Pudding (page 140) in advance and refrigerate.

2. Prepare Meat Loaf (page 63) in loaf pan.

3. Prepare Scalloped Potatoes (page 41) in another loaf pan.

4. Unwrap 10-oz. pkg. of frozen vegetables and place in serving dish.

5. Insert shelf in oven. Place Meat Loaf and Potatoes on shelf and vegetable on the floor of the oven.

6. Microwave on High for 20:00-25:00 (16:40-20:00) minutes, or until meat loaf reaches 135°F.

Beef Roast
Roasted Potatoes
Carrots
Salad
Fresh Mixed Fruit
Brownies

Preparation Time: 50 minutes
6-8 servings

1. Prepare Brownies (pages 123) several hours in advance and set aside.

2. Follow instructions for Chuck Roast (page 61) by combining roast, potatoes, and carrots in a cooking bag with juice, seasoning, and thickening.

3. While dinner is cooking, set table, prepare salad, and mixed fruit.

Pork Chops
Baked Potatoes
Vegetable
Salad
Tapioca Pudding

Preparation Time: 30 minutes
4 servings

1. Prepare Tapioca Pudding (page 142) several house in advance and refrigerate.

2. Place 4 Pork Chops that weigh about ½ pound each in a glass baking dish. Cover with plastic wrap or place in cooking bag.

3. Scrub and pierce 4 medium-sized Baking Potatoes.

4. Unwrap 10-oz. pkg. of a frozen vegetable and place in serving dish.

5. Insert shelf in oven. Place Pork Chops and Potatoes on shelf, and vegetable on the floor of the oven.

6. Microwave for 20:00-25:00 (16:40-20:50) minutes at 70%, or until pork chops reach 170 °F.

Note: Meats with similar weights or cooking times can be substituted for the pork chops; for instance, two pounds of spare ribs or chicken can be used.

Chicken
Stuffing
Mixed Vegetable
Salad
Quick Cherry Crunch

1. Prepare Quick Cherry Crunch (page 138) several hours in advance and set aside.

2. Prepare favorite Stuffing in shallow baking pan.

3. Arrange Chicken pieces prepared for cooking (see page 82 for ideas) on top of Stuffing.

4. Unwrap 10-oz. pkg. frozen mixed vegetables.

5. Place Chicken and Stuffing on shelf in microwave, and place mixed vegetables on the floor of the oven.

6. Microwave for suggested cooking time for Chicken (see page 82).

7. Set table, prepare salad and dessert.

Chicken
Rice
Vegetable
Salad
Cupcakes

Preparation Time: 25 minutes
4 servings

1. Place 2 lbs. Chicken pieces on microwave-safe baking dish. Sprinkle with browning powder or paprika. Cover with plastic wrap or place in cooking bag.

2. Combine 1 cup Rice, 2 cups water, 1 Tbsp. butter, and 1 tsp. salt in large covered casserole.

3. Unwrap 10-oz. pkg. of a frozen vegetable and place in serving dish.

4. Insert shelf in oven. Place Chicken and Rice on shelf and vegetable on the floor of the oven.

5. Microwave on High for 20:00-25:00 (16:40-20:50) minutes, or until Rice is tender and Chicken comes away from the bones.

6. Set table, prepare salad, and mix Cupcakes (see page 115). Bake just as you serve the main course.

Chicken Cordon Bleu
Potato Stuffing
Green Bean Bake
Cole Slaw
Chocolate Mousse

Preparation Time: 50-60 minutes
6-8 servings

1. Prepare cole slaw and Chocolate Mousse (page 143). (These are best if prepared a few hours ahead of serving time.)

2. Prepare Potato Stuffing (page 43) in shallow baking pan.

3. Arrange prepared Chicken pieces (page 82) on top of Stuffing.

4. Prepare Green Bean Bake (page 38).

5. Place Chicken and Stuffing on shelf in microwave and place Green Bean Casserole on the floor of the oven.

6. Microwave on High for 10:00 (8:20) minutes, reversing the positions of the two casseroles halfway through the cooking time.

Note: This is an ideal meal to serve to guests because it can be prepared ahead of time, heated at meal time, then served right from the oven without much last-minute preparation.

Fish
Mashed Potatoes
Stewed Tomatoes
Salad
Lemon Chiffon Pie

1. Prepare Lemon Chiffon Pie (page 134) several hours in advance and refrigerate.

2. Prepare Mashed Potatoes (page 41). Cover and set aside.

3. Prepare Stewed Tomatoes (use favorite recipe). Cover and set aside.

4. Arrange Fish in baking dish and prepare as desired (see pages 93-97).

5. Place Fish on shelf in microwave and place Potatoes and Tomatoes on the floor of the oven to reheat as the Fish cooks.

6. Microwave for suggested cooking time for Fish.

7. Set table and prepare salad and beverage.

Breaded Fish Fillets
Twice-Baked Potatoes
Green Bean Bake
Peach Crumb Pie

1. Bake Pie shell (page 132).

2. Prepare Pie filling and bake (page 132).

3. Bake Potatoes (page 35) and set aside.

4. Cook Beans (page 38) and set aside.

5. Prepare Potatoes for second baking.

6. Finish Bean casserole in oven, cover, and set aside.

7. Preheat browning dish and cook Fish Fillets. Set aside.

8. Finish Potatoes.

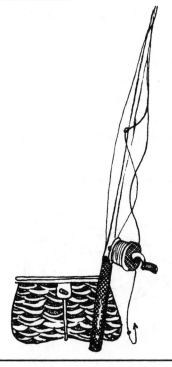

Spaghetti
Meat Sauce
Tossed Salad
Garlic Bread
Ice Cream

Preparation Time: 25 minutes
6-8 servings

1. Prepare Ice Cream (page 145).

2. Partially cook Spaghetti Noodles
(see page 54).

3. Prepare tossed salad and garlic bread
while noodles cook. Prepare garlic bread by
slicing a loaf of Italian bread and spreading
it with garlic butter made by blending
¼ lb. butter with 1 clove garlic. Wrap loaf
in napkin and set aside.

4. Prepare sauce (page 70) or heat a jar of
your favorite spaghetti sauce by placing
probe in the jar and heating to 130 °F. Pour
sauce over noodles and toss gently. Return
to oven and microwave on High for 6:00
(5:00) more minutes. Top with Parmesan
cheese.

5. Microwave Garlic Bread on High for
60 (50) seconds.

*Note: Spaghetti squash can be substituted for
the noodles.*

Bacon and Cheese Omelet
Cinnamon Rolls
Frozen Orange Drink

1. Sauté Bacon in microwave (page 73).

2. Prepare Caramel Nut Sticky Buns (page
109), or heat frozen Cinnamon Rolls. Cover
and set aside.

3. Prepare Omelet (page 25).

4. While Omelet cooks, prepare Frozen
Orange Drink (page 170).

Stuffed Hot Dogs
Cream of Broccoli Soup
Apple Crisp

1. Prepare Apple Crisp (page 137) several
hours in advance and set aside.

2. Microwave bacon for half the normal
cooking time (see page 73).

3. Prepare white sauce (page 18).

4. Stuff and wrap Hot Dogs with cheese
and bacon.

5. Add Broccoli to white sauce and finish
Soup (page 48).

6. Cook Hot Dogs (page 79).

7. Serve Hot Dogs in rolls with Soup.

Tips

- To soften ½ lb. butter or cream cheese, microwave in a glass dish on High for 30-45 (25-38) seconds.

- To melt 2 Tbsp. butter or margarine, microwave in a glass dish on High for 30 (25) seconds.

- For crisp bread crumbs, microwave 1 cup in 2 Tbsp. melted butter on High for 60 (50) seconds.

- Crisp stale chips or crackers by microwaving between paper towels on High for 20-30 (17-25) seconds.

- Soften hard brown sugar by placing it in a glass dish with a wedge of apple or slice of bread. Microwave on High for 30 (25) seconds per cup.

- To toast nuts, spread in single layer and microwave on High for 3:00 (2:30) minutes per cup, stirring every minute.

- To melt 8 ozs. of chocolate, microwave on High for 60 (50) seconds. Stir, then repeat procedure at 30 (25)-second intervals until chocolate is melted. Always be sure to stir before adding more time.

- Microwave tomatoes on High for 30 (25) seconds for easy peeling.

- Microwave frozen concentrate in paper or plastic containers on High for 30 (25) seconds to make mixing easier.

- Soften ice cream to custardy consistency by microwaving on High for 10-15 (8-13) seconds.

- Separate slices of frozen bacon easily by microwaving them on High for 15 (13) seconds.

- Reheat leftover pancakes, waffles, and sweet rolls for a quick, just-baked taste. Wrap in paper towel and microwave on High for 8-10 (7-8) seconds.

- Soften tortillas between paper towels. For 12 tortillas, microwave on High for 60 (50) seconds.

- Reheat leftover coffee for just-perked flavor. Microwave on High for 2:00 (1:40) minutes per cup.

- Instead of preparing a hot water bottle, microwave a wet washcloth in a heavy plastic bag for 30 (25) seconds.

- Use a Temperature Probe when liquids are to be at an exact temperature.

- Clean your oven by first microwaving a soapy dishcloth on High for 30 (25) seconds. Then wipe the oven with the clean cloth.

Index

About the Author

Maryann Zepp, Seattle, Washington, is an experienced instructor in the use of the microwave oven. She is a graduate of Drexel University in home economics education. She has also studied nutrition and the culinary arts at Immaculata College, The Pennsylvania State University, and Johnson and Wales. A former high school teacher and baker owner, she has developed products and recipes for major food companies in Pennsylvania, Ohio, and Washington.